7/21/23

Soul of a Democrat

Soul of a Democrat

THE SEVEN CORE IDEALS
THAT MADE OUR PARTY—
AND OUR COUNTRY—GREAT

THOMAS B. RESTON

ALL
POINTS
BOOKS

SOUL OF A DEMOCRAT. Copyright © 2018 by Thomas B. Reston. All rights reserved. Printed in the United States of America. For information, address St. Martin's Press, 175 Fifth Avenue, New York, NY 10010.

All Points Books is an imprint of St. Martin's Press.

www.allpointsbooks.com

Designed by Steven Seighman

The Library of Congress Cataloging-in-Publication Data is available upon request.

ISBN 978-1-250-17605-9 (hardcover)
ISBN 978-1-250-17607-3 (ebook)

Our books may be purchased in bulk for promotional, educational, or business use. Please contact your local bookseller or the Macmillan Corporate and Premium Sales Department at 1-800-221-7945, extension 5442, or by email at MacmillanSpecialMarkets@macmillan.com.

First Edition: May 2018

10 9 8 7 6 5 4 3 2 1

This book is dedicated to my father

JAMES B. RESTON
of
The New York Times

Journalist
Patriot
Amiable Skeptic
Expositor of Democracy
Immigrant
Devoted Parent

With Abiding Love

CONTENTS

Soul of a Democrat

HAS THE DEMOCRATIC PARTY LOST ITS SOUL?

Here—in the answer to this single question—lies the master key that opens the way for Democrats to return to power.

If the Democrats find the answers to all their other questions, about what the details of their policy proposals should be, about how to find the candidates and raise the money and get the voters to the polls—even about who the Republicans are—and yet cannot locate their soul, they will fail themselves, and fail the country.

To get back to power, the Democrats first have to get back to their own soul.

The Democratic Soul: Deep politics is my theme. I am interested in the civic faiths that remain and underpin everything else, the everything-else that is the stuff of temporary political maneuver. I am talking about beliefs so elementary and vital that they have defined the Democrats—have answered the questions of who the Democrats really are, and why, and how and why they differ from their opponents—down the generations through all the cycles of American history, from Thomas Jefferson reading alone in his study at Monticello right up to the moment you hold this book in your hands. I am talking about how to achieve perspective on today's political struggle. I am talking about the roots and anchors of the Democratic Party.

This, therefore, is a book about the fundamentals of politics, and the fundamentals do not go away. Yet the truth is that today, these fundamentals are the very things that too many Democrats have lost sight of. Has the Democratic Party lost its soul? It is a question of groundwork politics, and it contains many other profound questions about the meaning of democracy in America today. These turn out to be serious questions, and very tough ones. Democrats have had trouble answering the questions this book will raise. These are questions, in fact, that they have ceased even to ask of themselves.

And this is the reason why, in 2016, when the Democrats could no longer tell their fellow citizens—in emotional and simple and coherent and blunt and honest words—what their own meaning was for today's politics, these unanswered questions finally, after some five decades of drift, sank the Democrats—at all levels of our national life—and opened the door not only to a Donald Trump presidency, but also to the prospect of a fundamental realignment of America's two great political parties, with the Democratic Party in permanent opposition, and in permanent minority.

This worries me a great deal, and it is the reason why I wrote this book. I am a Democrat. I have been a Democrat all my life. I have never voted for a Republican. I am a Democrat today, and I shall remain a Democrat. I am not about to leave, and I do not claim that my party has left me. I like my party and the people in it. I wrote this book because I want to see Democrats succeed. Rather than offering specific campaign advice, this book presents the perennial themes and values of our party that individual candidates may apply in different ways, at different times, in different parts of the country.

IN SEARCH OF THE DEMOCRATIC SOUL

When the voters visited calamity upon the Democrats on the night of November 8, 2016, and we had been thrown out of the White House, checked in the House of Representatives, staggered in the Senate, a majority on the Supreme Court was suddenly and frighteningly placed in play, and, catastrophically, we had been expelled en masse from the statehouses and governors' mansions so that we remained in control of only six out of fifty state governments in the entire nation, I thought, surely, now, Democrats will pause to consider who we are and where we've gone wrong; surely we will mount a searching re-examination of what our party really stands for, down deep; and maybe if the self-assessment is honest enough, we will find new ways to recapture the trust of our countrymen.

It never happened.

Instead, after the election was over, Democrats returned to exactly the same strategy that had brought us defeat in November. We focused exclusively on the man who had beat us. He became, for us, a monomania. It was an easy way to unite the Party, for there were very few Democrats who liked Trump, but it was too easy. It was important, of course, to take into account the meaning of Trump's election as president. It is the duty of an opposition to oppose, so yes, the Democrats needed to mobilize in order to bring ourselves back; yes, the Democrats needed to resist. I, too, am a resister.

But in fact, the result of all this is that the political conversation of the nation has coarsened way beyond the experience or comprehension of any generation of living Americans, and it has hurt the country. It is the political conversation itself that is important. The conversation is the measure of the civic health of our country. The passions of our times have become intense because of Donald Trump's enormities. We are all now partakers in the conversation that he engineered, and regrettably, this includes Democrats as well as Republicans. He framed the conversation. We argued it on his terms. The alarming thing is that in the period after the Republicans took control of the federal government in January 2017, Democrats often succumbed to the temptation to sink to the level of the pronouncements emanating from the Trump White House. And so, sometimes, it seemed as if any argument, any means, any last-chance bitter epithet could get the green light from us, as well as from him. In our rush to naked partisanship, we could cast aside our deeper instincts, our higher principles, and our own broader hopes for the country. Too often, we allowed ourselves to become corrupted by the discourse. Our own sometimes eager and acrid and repetitive contributions helped to debase a conversation so unworthy of, and so insulting to, the American people. There was a different way—a better and more effective way—open to us, and we didn't take it.

Somehow, the Republic will survive President Trump, no matter the length of his tenure in office. This, too, shall pass. My argument here is about something more lasting, more difficult, and more important than Donald Trump. My argument is about the *meaning of the Democratic Party*. This is the question that can no longer be put off. This question has to be faced up to, right now. And to answer this question, we must look to ourselves. The first thing we need to do is pick up the mirror.

In thinking so obsessively about Trump and the Republicans, the Democrats missed the opportunity to think seriously about themselves. What truly matters is this: the problems that are fundamental for the Democrats lie within the Democratic Party itself. These problems were there long before Trump. They will remain long after Trump. They cannot be magically erased, even should the Democrats score a landslide victory in a single set of off-year elections. They are problems that could prove life-threatening for the Democratic Party, philosophically as well as numerically, unless the Democrats come to terms with them. And as opposed to the doings of Trump and the Grand Old Party, these are questions that Democrats have absolute control over. Yet these were the very problems the Democrats chose to ignore. All of this was a major failure of Democratic imagination. The consequences for our party—and for our country—are ominous.

The search for the Democratic soul begins with the obvious question: Is there even such a thing as the Democratic soul? My answer is an emphatic yes, and this whole book is a meditation on the different, and often conflicting, parts of our soul, and what has happened to it, and what the implications are for our politics today.

The first thing to say is that the soul of the Democratic Party is not to be found in the passing policies of the Democrats, the things that come and go, like low tariffs or Free Silver or Obamacare. Our policies are important—yes, we should fight for a higher minimum wage, and yes, a lot of Democrats believe we should have fought harder for single-payer healthcare—but our policies do not define our soul. Our soul is different, qualitatively distinct, and this is critical. Our soul runs infinitely deeper than our policies. It lasts longer. It is more difficult to budge. There is a mystery to it. It is more powerful. But it has precious little to do with the footnotes of policies, or the effectiveness of public administration, or efficiency in government, or any of the how-tos of politics—themes Democrats seem to have emphasized a lot in recent times.

Instead, soul dwells in instinct. And instinct is directly and crucially related to the concept of political *purpose*. In politics, the purpose of what you are trying to do is more important than how you try to accomplish it. There's going to be a lot more in this book about this idea, but let me tell a couple of stories right here in the beginning to illustrate the kind of thing I mean.

Probably the most valuable political asset the Democratic Party has ever held in its hands can be summed up in just four words: "for the little guy." We took resolute and even defiant possession of these four words almost two hundred years ago. Andrew Jackson's ascent to power in 1829 fixes more than just the foundation date of the modern Democratic Party. The very instant of his administration's birth reveals what allowed us to solidify our domination of America during the first half of the nineteenth century and, even more important, marked the Democratic Party for all time thereafter with its innate political character. Here is a story about political soul.

Tellingly, Democrats used to recount the tale of Andrew Jackson's inauguration night with more relish and pride than they seem to muster today. This is the old yarn about how mobs of backwoods ruffians, high on triumph and corn whiskey, overran the White House, smashing the crockery and punch bowls—but smashing, also, theretofore unquestioned assumptions about power, and who was to have it. It was a new day, for Jackson had brought the New West to power, setting the old high-and-mighty eastern establishment firmly aside. And—critically—he had linked the westerners in political harness to those who were laboring in the burgeoning industries of urban America. Everywhere, albeit within the understandings of his own times, he worked implacably to expand the franchise, thereby earning the devoted political loyalty of the Common Man.

This is the coalition that has sustained the Democratic Party throughout American history. The people at work in the big cities and on the land and in the small towns; the people standing up for themselves, coming out of the labor union movement; the immigrants who uprooted their lives and came from abroad looking for the main chance, or for any chance; the people in their millions who fueled the urban machines that piled up our massive majorities; the people who gave it to you straight from the shoulder, who were bored by the fancy arguments, and who were determined to find out, instead, whether you were on their side, or whether you were not. These are the people who saved the Democrats even when we were going under—when, in all justice, we probably deserved to go under—amidst our post–Civil War disgrace. They are the ones who delivered us our victories—and, even more important, they are the ones who imprinted the Democratic Party with its abiding purposes and philosophical meanings.

It is this coalition that the Jacksonian Democracy first forged, of urban and rural working people—and that Democrats have continued to expand since that long-ago time—which has allowed us to outlast all of our rivals throughout American history:

the Federalists, the Whigs, the Know Nothings, the Populists, the Dixiecrats, the Progressives—all gone now.

This Jacksonian coalition of ours largely accounts for the name Americans of past generations so often applied to us, sometimes with affection, and sometimes in rue: Old Indestructible.

Another story in political soul: John Nance Garner of Texas was Franklin Roosevelt's vice president during FDR's first two terms. Garner was a salty, archconservative, states'-rights man, profoundly skeptical of big, centralized government programs. During the early months of the New Deal, the cabinet was meeting to discuss the emergency and what to do about it. The department heads were calculating the intricate and immediate political pros and cons of some policy proposal, debating whether to move or not to move, and finally, from the end of the table, the vice president spoke up: "Mr. President," Garner said, "I think that when we were campaigning we sort of made promises that we would do something for the poorer kind of people, and I think we have to do something for them. We have to remember them. We have to take account of that." Garner then went on to endorse immediate federal relief aid for the desperate and suffering.

FDR took note and was impressed. Something more profound than political calculation or keeping promises was moving his temperamentally conservative vice president. It was deep Jacksonian political instinct that was reaching up from somewhere underneath to guide his political course and overcome his traditional reluctance to act.

You heard it all the time on the street, a generation ago, when people wanted to explain why they supported us: "The Democrats—they're for the little guy. The Common Man." When was the last time you heard this said?

There are other bedrock Democratic credos beyond the little guy and the Common Man, and this book is going to go into them all. But for the moment, the point is this: because the American people felt instincts like these to be powerfully at work in us, they felt that we would be dependable, that they could rely on us, that we would try very hard, somehow and despite all the difficulties and day-to-day pressures, to remain true to our fundamental purposes. That's why they took us to their hearts. Our party was about something. It meant something. We were not just a political party; we were *the* party. We were America's political party.

We didn't talk publicly about having a soul, of course, but somehow, that's what it was about; that's what we had. We had a soul. And we've lost some of that now, in the eyes of our fellow citizens. All of it? No. We still understand and act on parts of our soul. But major parts of it? Yes. We've neglected or turned our face from important parts of our heritage, parts that once played decisive and honorable roles in establishing our political dominance of the nation. This doesn't mean that the Democratic soul has disappeared forever. I believe that our soul, in its entirety, remains. But it remains for us to uncover it, and then to recover it.

So, this book is about big politics, the things that matter the most in the political struggle. And as Justice Oliver Wendell Holmes Jr. once said: "It seems to me that at this time we need education in the obvious more than investigation of the obscure."

THE EDUCATION OF A DEMOCRAT

My own political education began in the American South. In fact, I was only a boy on the day I decided to give myself to the political struggle. It happened in Front Royal, Virginia, out in the Shenandoah Valley, in late September 1958. Virginia had closed the public high school there to avoid the racial integration that federal courts had ordered. I watched it happen. I didn't understand it, but I knew it was wrong. And I never forgave the men who did it. Eight years later, I would come back to Virginia to fight the people who had closed the public schools. Those people were Democrats, and by then, I was a Democrat too.

I spent a decade battling through Virginia politics, along the way getting elected in convention as Secretary of the State Democratic Party. As I organized and stumped my way across the Old Dominion in those days, down the country roads, inside the courthouses, in the heart of the cities, and across the endless suburbs, the whole political culture of the state was unraveling. What I was watching was a Democratic Party coming to recognize that its old ways of believing and doing things were played out, a party caught between yesterday and tomorrow, without a sure and guiding philosophy. The Party wasn't hanging together, with conservatives and liberals both streaming for the exits.

There weren't a lot of us who stuck by the Party, and among those who remained, there were plenty of Democrats whom I disagreed with, but I learned that it was not my business to demand perfect motives from my fellow partisans. We needed their votes. In time, I would change, but I became, for a while, a live-and-let-live Democrat, that's all, without giving it much more thought than that. It was in Virginia that I developed the basic instinct for practical politics that I have carried with me ever since. I'm operational: I like to win, and I'm interested in how to do that. But even so, underneath my operational veneer, the thing I mostly took away from that decade was that our lack of workable, reliable, fundamental bearings back then made for tough politics in Virginia. It makes for tough politics again today, nationally.

My political world began to get bigger. I went to work for a time for the governor of Maryland in the old State House in Annapolis. There I watched him create a modern state government with a streamlined bureaucracy, and he got it done by pulling together his legislature. The Maryland General Assembly included some of the same kinds of Democrats that I recognized from my experience across the river in Virginia: Democrats out of the small towns and faraway counties, Democrats from the smart and sophisticated suburbs, but now different Democrats, too, from the big and sometimes ugly machine that ran Baltimore—gaudy and extravagant politicians who were loads of fun, but who were utterly serious about getting the things they needed for their people. The legislature was filled with officeholders who stayed loyal to the essence of who they were and what they came out of, and a lot of the time they didn't understand each other very well, but they spoke their minds freely and bluntly, and then cut the deals that made things work. I liked them, and I liked this bigger party of mine, even though it was plenty hard for me to make sense of it.

The Democratic Party, I was coming to learn, is like a civics laboratory, an elementary-school classroom in how the larger politics of our country functions. We are not a liberal party that opposes a conservative party. We are a party that contains a multiplicity of interests that opposes a party that, traditionally at least, has been dominated by a single interest. To learn how to maneuver inside the Democratic Party, therefore, is to learn how to operate beyond the Party as well, in the broader public realm—even to learn how to govern. Our government is a system of checks and balances among three branches. The Democratic

Party is a system of checks and balances that must accommodate an almost endless series of power centers. It offers everyday lessons in how to get along with different kinds of people. It is the manifold diversity of our coalition—diversities of ideals, ideas, values, ethnicities, geographies, religions, interests—that is our glory, and our chief problem.

And then, for me, came the national presidential campaigns, eight of them in all, with whole geographies in play, and the calculations were much more complex: Could we hold the Upper Midwest? What did we have to do to have a chance in the Border States? Some of these drives were winners, some losers; some rolled out in placid days, and some—like our desperate struggle in 1968—unfolded amidst bitter divisions in the nation: that year, civil rights and Vietnam. I sailed under three flags during the presidential primaries in 1968: first, for Robert Kennedy, who was shot; then, for Eugene McCarthy, who went down in the most chaotic Democratic convention of the past hundred years; and finally, for Vice President Hubert Humphrey, who lost by a hair. September 1968 was gruesome for Humphrey and his loyalist Democrats, with angry union workers bolting to Governor George Wallace of Alabama, running as an independent, and with proud and prickly antiwar crusaders sitting unapproachably on the sidelines.

For the last several weeks of that '68 fight, I traveled with Humphrey as he vaulted the nation. I was a baggage-smasher on his campaign plane. I got to watch him in front of every conceivable sort of crowd, in private as well as public, all different kinds of Americans—Americans of every color and accent, from every part of the country, insiders and outsiders, people who liked him and people who most assuredly did not, hawks and doves, earnest good-government types. Late one night, just before the election, we rolled into Hudson County, New Jersey, where 180 we've-seen-it-all machine types sat silently on the platform waiting for him to arrive (many of them, I was told, from the County Mosquito Control Board). One of them whispered to me: "Don't worry. He'll do all right here. We're sticking with him."

The thing that impressed me back then during those frenetic weeks, but impresses me even more now, was the way Humphrey dealt with the crowds that swelled and swelled as his fight caught fire with Election Day approaching. His rallies were like revival meetings. He preached the old-time gospel of the New Deal to them. Nobody had to tell him who he was or what he should say. He hardly ever read a speech or even read from notes. He spoke from the heart. He knew what he was about.

And he dealt with all the crowds in exactly the same way. He told them all the same thing, no matter who they were. He didn't try to slice and dice his various constituencies with tailor-made special pleading, thereby isolating his supporters one from another. No. He insisted on making one argument for everyone—an argument that could unite his wildly disparate following and hold them together. In the end, of course, it was Nixon who won, but not by much: Humphrey damn near pulled it off.

For a young man standing in the crowd, watching him and listening to him doggedly and joyously pleading the cause for which he stood, the Democratic campaign of 1968 carried profound lessons about ideas and their influence over the destiny of politics. I began to think: Could there be a politics that would celebrate, instead of smother, the rough-and-tumble of genuinely opposed instincts and interests inside our broad and fractious coalition, and yet bring it together within a framework of

American idealisms that were honorably homegrown by the Democrats themselves?

Later, things got even more complicated for me. Eight years on, I went into the federal government as a political appointee, into the Foreign Service at the State Department, and without, at first, really thinking it through, I carried my Democratic politics out into the world. My job was to explain in public what the United States was doing abroad amidst the endless complexities of diplomatic, military, and political maneuver. I made it my constant endeavor to place the details of our foreign-policy tactics into the framework of American interests—and values— and a lot of those values I had learned at the knee of my political party here at home.

I have been at this for a long time now—long enough to have seen my political life get cut in two. For the first half of my life, the political story that the Democratic Party told the country— essentially, it was Franklin Roosevelt's New Deal—was able to set the boundary lines of the national debate, and by doing so, we were able to organize and even to dominate the power struggle. Ronald Reagan challenged our political paradigm outright in 1980, and he changed the country's conversation. This one act made the starkest difference to Democratic prospects, and not for the better, because since 1980, the Republicans have controlled the underlying story line of American politics. And thus, no matter which party held the White House, the Republican Party has dominated the second half of my life.

What Reagan did in 1980 did not change my political views, but he changed the way I thought about politics. I realized I had to look for deeper reasons to explain why we were having so much trouble gaining traction. This political truth is stabbingly on point once again today, after the election of 2016—for we may now be facing a new inflection point in American politics, like the one Reagan and the Republicans engineered with so much zeal and tenacity, and with so much success, in 1980.

All these lessons from my past formed the political instincts I hold today, and I have poured them into this book, which is really a guidebook for the path that leads through the Democratic soul and the Democratic mind and toward the future—and a new Democratic Party.

THE GREAT WANDERING OF THE
MODERN DEMOCRATS

At the end of the Second World War, Democrats instinctively understood each other and the country, and the nation understood us. Everyone recognizes that this is no longer true today. The Party has gone astray. After 1948, the Democrats began their great wandering of the modern age. We have yet to emerge. We set forth in clarity and vigor. We arrive in confusion. Democrats have wandered because we have allowed our minds to wander. To find our way home, and back to power, we must refocus our minds and consider our soul. That is the first and fundamental problem of our politics today.

There has been a decades-long decoupling of the presidential candidates of the Democratic Party and the party that gave them its nomination, but even more ominously, there has been a decoupling of the Democratic Party and its essential meanings for the life of the nation. And if you let go of your own purpose and meaning in politics, you have handed your opponents the most valuable advantage there is in the political struggle. You have invited them to seize control of the terms of the political debate. They will then control the rules of the game, and their fundamental ideas will decide its outcome. Or maybe they will seize control of your own originating ideals that you've lost sight of and impose their updated interpretation on them, and make them theirs instead of yours. When this happens, you are at a permanent disadvantage until you can figure out how to change the basic philosophical terms of the contest. You have arrived at the exact spot where the Democrats find themselves today. You are living in the aftermath of the 2016 elections.

John F. Kennedy was the last Democratic presidential nominee to actually campaign for the office as a Democrat. He printed the Party's name all over his literature, and he talked about it constantly in his speeches throughout 1960. Not a single one of our subsequent nominees has followed JFK's lead. For the Party's rank and file, that's well over half a century of being stashed out of sight on the back shelf.

Yet even with Jack Kennedy, there was a studied calculation and a cool design to the relations he had with his political party. His election had been a near thing, and afterward, he faced an entrenched southern bloc in Congress, so he saw that he needed the Party and such party discipline as was available to him. But he did only enough to keep his side of the bargain, because politics for him was not about party. It was about power and getting things done and doing what you had to do, and if the Party helped, fine, and if the Party didn't help, well, that was fine too; it was all the same to him. He was not a sentimentalist.

And when he became president, Kennedy's principal reliance and loyalty could sometimes seem to run more to the intellectual elite than it did to the Democratic Party itself. He was at ease with bright, highly refined, educated people, and it was their company he sought out more than the raw, less-refined, street-smart barons of his gritty political coalition. Rank-and-file Democrats put a lot of emotion behind him—they felt the electromagnetic field surrounding him—but they felt the distance, too. He kept to himself, by inclination and temperament. Many modern Democrats, including Presidents Clinton and Obama, revere him, yet his legacy is a tapestry of ironies. He remains a study in personality, not in ideas, despite the historical turn of his mind and his intellectual curiosity. Thus, he is the classic exemplar of why so many today repeat the blasé mantra of "I vote for the candidate, not the party."

Lyndon Johnson was a throwback. He started out as a New Dealer when rural Texas sent him to Congress at age twenty-nine, and that's what he remained until the day he left the White House three decades later. He was a grandiose man, and his incredible political mind governed amidst grandiosities: more programs, more agencies, more acronyms, more money. At bedrock, he believed profoundly in the good that government could do for people. Johnson was a dyed-in-the-wool Democrat, to be sure, but his greediness for the big win always caused him to downplay his party affiliation. He did not portray himself officially as a Democrat when he campaigned for election in 1964. He suppressed partisanship in his dealings with Congress. His oozing legislative incantation of "come, let us reason together" was at once sincere and cynical—not to mention brilliantly successful—as he manhandled Republicans as well as Democrats to produce his lopsided victories on the Hill. The spotlight was on LBJ as legislative sorcerer bringing his Great Society to life. The star of the show was larger than life. But the Democratic Party was largely absent. He served the tangible Great

Society. He discarded the Party. It was Lyndon Baines Johnson who took the credit.

With Johnson, you always had the sense that he knew what he wanted, but with his successor, Jimmy Carter, you had the sense that he was never quite sure. People said he was a fiscal conservative and a social liberal, but it was hard to figure out when he would favor one side or the other, should they collide, as inevitably they did. In the hands of a master politician like Franklin Roosevelt, this capacity for unpredictability can be an advantage. It has been remarked of Napoleon, for instance, that when he ceased to astonish, he began to decline.

Carter was not a master politician. In deciding how to govern, he explicitly ruled out politics as usual. He decided to take each problem as it came, consider it substantively and deliberately on its own merits, and finally do the right thing. In a way, the president organized his first administration as if it had been a second administration. But this searching for each new right answer began to unsettle the public. There was a sense that his policies weren't really hanging together. This can be a problem in politics, and it became a problem for President Carter. He made people uneasy. He made even people who respected him uneasy. People weren't sure where he was coming from, or where he was going. And often he seemed to be operating on his own.

Carter had been denied the undoubted benefits of a divisive election based on substance. His overriding campaign theme in 1976, in the wake of Nixon's Watergate scandal, was basic, decent, clean government. He delivered on that promise, but somehow, he could never find refuge in the Democratic Party's own traditional wisdom as a homing beacon for his administration's policies. Whereas Jack Kennedy's view of the Party had been unsentimental, twenty years later Jimmy Carter's stance could sometimes seem to verge on disdain. When he stepped down from office and began to do oral histories, he used phrases like "the biggest handicap I had," which "pulled us down a good bit in the polls," when referring to his party. The former president was quite objective about himself in all this, volunteering that his relationship with the Democratic Party was "not particularly good," and then adding, almost curtly, that changing that relationship was "not a burning commitment or interest of mine."

One result of this political wandering was that the American public became more confused about the Democratic Party and what its purposes really were. Indeed, the political jujitsu that Ronald Reagan performed on the Democrats in 1980—an intellectual whipping that produced the most profound paradigm shift in American politics in half a century—represented the triumph of clarity over confusion. "Government is not the solution to our problem," Reagan announced on taking office, "government is the problem." This childish turn of phrase would have appalled Thomas Jefferson, not to mention FDR, but it did provide the public with a clear standard by which to judge the actions Reagan's administration would take. People understood what he was setting out to do. He brought millions of disenchanted Democrats into the Republican Party.

A dozen years of the exceptionally clear-minded Reagan critique of New Deal Democratic politics left our partisans scattered and demoralized. When Bill Clinton arrived in 1992, he figured that the solution was to pull the Democratic Party as far back as he could into the moderate center. His instinct was defensive, but it succeeded, in a limited sense. Clinton was a realist. He moved carefully, marginally. He did not approach his political problems as a matter of strategy. There was no grand design of fundamental political principle. There was no deep consideration

or reconsideration of fundamental Democratic Party philosophy as an independently standing positive force in the life of
the country. Instead, there were tactics. Indeed, this is what Bill
Clinton seemed to be all about: the tactics of policy.

He took the world as he found it. He charted out rival
political compass points—Reagan and Thatcher on the right,
European socialists on the left—and the course he would plot
in foreign policy was "the third way": right in the center. At
home, in domestic policy, it was called "triangulation," as he
steered precisely down the center between the extremes of
the Democratic and Republican parties. He was in no way passive, but he finessed his way between other people's big ideas.

When it was all over, we seemed better positioned for the day
at hand, ready for the next necessary pirouette, but without a
sure sense of our own rootedness, and somehow it seemed fair
to raise the question of just how serious the Democrats were being about all this. Had we developed a new, genuine, instinctive moderation, or were we merely adrift amidst the pressures
of the moment? With a completely different political temperament from Jimmy Carter's, Bill Clinton may have raised the very
same specter before the public that Carter had: Democratic un-
dependability.

Barack Obama began with a different instinct. More so than
Kennedy, Carter, or Clinton, he understood the pulling power
of deep, emotional ideas in politics, and he understood quite well
how to tap into them, and he did just that when he first ran for
president in 2008. He may be the greatest orator the Democrats
have produced since Woodrow Wilson, but after he won his election, he seemed to change. The language he used virtually all of
the time as a governing official was not rhetorical at all; instead,
it was marked through and through with the language of the

professoriate: intelligent, lucid, hedged, cautious, multisyllabic, detailed, didactic. As president, Obama made the case for his programs, but it was a case in the footnotes, in the details. The details he had down, cold. But the relationship between the details of his policies and their political or philosophical context was unclear or simply absent altogether. What Obama failed to do—perhaps even failed to try to do—was to connect his policies to the deep wellsprings of his party's mission, and to offer a plausible story line as to how they could be made to fit together in principle, and work together as a matter of practical governing.

If Jimmy Carter was the one who seemed to puzzle his party the most among the post–World War II Democratic presidents, surely Barack Obama ran him a close second. Endless was the private speculation among Democrats as to who the "real" Obama was, and what his true governing instinct was. His supporters sensed that he had the ability to put things into perspective for them and for the larger national community, yet the president rarely seemed to come through. More and more, he returned to what he thought he was best at: the details of his work governing the nation.

Obama is interesting because of the genuine, palpable excitement he generated in the very beginning. He showed that there was something deep inside the Democrats, longing to be touched again, something they had not felt in their bones since Truman in 1948. Every once in a while, President Obama spoke to the yearning of the nation, but ultimately he couldn't, or wouldn't, mobilize the political potential of that yearning. Barack Obama became a kind of false dawn to the Democrats, but he did show that there was a real dawn out there, waiting to be captured—and worth the prize.

THE POLITICS OF DEMOCRATIC ILLUSION

"Old Indestructible"—today? Somehow today, our party doesn't seem so stable, sure of itself, instinctive for its mission, or confident of its permanence so as to justify a moniker like Old Indestructible. Today, Old Indestructible, which Americans once took almost as a cliché, has become a question mark.

This book is written out of a profound conviction and a very real fear. The conviction is that we have disregarded and devalued the power that ideas and ideals can exert over the destiny of the political struggle; the fear is that we cannot recover and break out unless we clear the Democratic mind of those illusions that block our ability to imagine a new Democratic Party that can bring us back to power.

This book is an argument. It is an argument against people who claim that the Democratic Party doesn't matter anymore; people who look only to the 2016 presidential campaign for the cause of our troubles; people who say that our own failings are always somebody else's fault; people who believe that all we need is to get back to normal; people who try to convince us that our real enemies are other Democrats who don't agree 100 percent with their own views; people who think that our experts and consultants will save us; people who act as if policies equal politics; people who imagine that we can understand and encompass and govern the nation by focusing only on ourselves; people who look at the fading Democratic working-class base as a numbers problem; and finally, most destructively of all, people who have the illusion that we are powerless to do anything to get ourselves out of the mess we're in. All of these people are trapped in today's politics of Democratic illusion. They need a way out.

The illusion that the Democratic Party doesn't matter anymore. The opposite is true. The Democratic Party matters more than ever. Its withering as an independently standing, palpable institutional presence is in large measure responsible for the climate that has encouraged the selfish, for-me-alone ambition that marks too many of our leaders and elected officials at the moment. The Party can help bring these people to heel. It has often operated this way in the past; it can do so again. The people who, in their presumption, imagine that they are on top need to be reminded who sent them into politics in the first place. It was the Democratic Party, and the Democratic Party does stand for something, and has the power to insist on accountability. The Party's very feebleness today represents an opportunity: the leadership is weak, and Democrats concerned about their party's slide—and, indeed, the nation's uncertain fate—should pour into the Democratic Party's structure now, at all levels, as they did in the 1950s and early 1970s, and reinvigorate a politics that has gone stale.

The illusion that the 2016 election is the problem that we must remedy. It isn't. "What went wrong in 2016?" is the wrong question to ask, and yields the wrong answers. Our problems go deeper than the Trump election. The problems of the Democratic Party did not arise overnight on November 8, 2016. They have been building at least since 1968, and in order to understand the problem of the Democratic future, one must see 2016 in the context of the long evolution that led up to it. Finger-pointing over the details of the 2016 calamity is not a reassessment. It's a distraction and a cop-out.

The illusion that it's always somebody else's fault. The sum and substance of the re-evaluation the Democrats began shortly after November 8, 2016, had precious little to do with the Democratic Party itself. It had to do with Donald Trump and the Republicans and the disgraceful campaign they waged. It focused on the dictator in the Kremlin and his leak-seeking confederates. It concerned the unwise and possibly even sinister decisions of the Federal Bureau of Investigation. It pointed to other people's racism and other people's sexism. It mired itself amidst the technicalities of computer servers and email accounts. It wondered why the pollsters were wrong. Yet the rank and file of the Democratic Party had no ability to control or even influence any of these issues. Of course Donald Trump's campaign amounted to political serpentry, but that should not have been surprising, and, more to the point, that was beyond our power. Our problem was to figure out who *we* were and how to win, and we showed ourselves incapable of either task. Democrats need to concentrate on what we can control, on our own jobs at hand. We need to put in the hard work to fashion our own future instead of rendering so many cost-free opinions about other people's actions and flaws.

The illusion that all we need to do is get back to normal. There was a time, of course, long ago, when Democrats held the loyalty of a clear majority of America's voters. Forget it: it's nowhere near true now. We are not living through some tiny time-blip that momentarily interrupts a long-stretching era when our party commands the political heights. In reality, the Democratic candidacies of 2016 represented the final intensification of an intellectual line in the Party's history that had already run into deep trouble. Our fellow citizens rejected what we were offering and withdrew the mandates they had given us, virtually across the board, from the White House on down. Nationwide, the 2016 election results brought our party just about to its lowest point in a century. The way back to Democratic dominance does not lead through the very recent past or some imagined land of political normalcy. The way back to power lies through a new approach that can heal the lacerations that have breached our traditionally dominant coalition, and make us whole and strong again.

The illusion that we are our own worst enemy. The truest of all the truisms of Democratic Party history is that not all Democrats agree about why they should be Democrats in the first place. Calls for party unity are persistent, but they have never been taken seriously in any precise sense, since everyone has always tacitly understood that to demand unity of conscience and instinct from Democrats is to believe in illusion. Oddly, this has begun to change recently, and some of the current rhetoric and backroom maneuver, aimed at enforcing a true unity, have reached alarming proportions. This is a gift to the Republicans. To denounce the senator from West Virginia for voting in favor of the interests of out-of-work coal miners serves no purpose, and shows no understanding of the larger ethos of the Democratic Party. All Democrats should find it natural that Massachusetts Democrats and Wyoming Democrats should be different. To deplore those differences is beside the point, merely too easy. The hard work is to invent the frameworks that can hold Democrats together, and thereby help each other, even in the face of interests and values that may seem, at first blush, to clash.

The illusion that our experts and consultants will save us. This is perhaps the most galling Democratic illusion of them all. We live today with a Democratic Party whose leadership has handed over our most important powers and functions to outside hirelings and paymasters. It was the outside experts and consultants who concocted the 2016 strategies they promised would bring us through, but took us down instead. They have sunk us in a "scientific" politics of focus groups, special-interest question-naires, money, algorithms, big data, and predictable pettinesses. They have digitized The People. The rank and file of the Party have taken too much advice of late from freelancers who are completely unfamiliar with local people and local conditions of life. The homegrown Party now needs to reassert control, and that means rank-and-file Democrats. Outside consultants need to be put firmly in their place. Local Democrats from the pre-cincts need to be deciding what the Party is and who it will run for office.

The illusion that policies are politics. Policies are critical, of course; ultimately, government expresses itself through poli-cies. And clearly, policies and politics are mutually dependent on each other. But the two are not the same thing. And the trouble is that a lot of Democrats today believe that they are, and conduct themselves accordingly. The code of Democratic poli-tics has become encrusted with policy prescriptions. The policy lingo isn't working with the public anymore. The public is de-manding something sturdier. It now behooves the Democrats to examine themselves closely: If the policy-equals-politics para-digm isn't working, why not? And what should we replace it with? The history of this particular illusion runs back for a hundred years through American history, and the heart of the Democratic Party is where this struggle has played itself out. It's time for Democrats to resolve it.

The illusion that we can govern or even begin to under-stand the nation by focusing only on ourselves. The reality is that the country is evenly divided. The illusion is that we can control the destiny of the country by making sure we are better at turning out our voters than they are at turning out theirs. This is not strategic politics; this is a hit-or-miss crapshoot where you have only a random chance of winning the close ones, which is what most of them are; and sometimes, even when you win the popular vote (2000, 2016), you still lose the election. Going back to our base is not enough. We need to get beyond our base. We need a strategy that can produce big, structural strides forward with the national electorate. We must seek a clearly enduring and stable majority of Americans that can consistently win for us and support what we do when in office.

Because politics is about more than getting to 50 percent plus one. Of course the people who voted Democratic recently are critical to us, and we must stay close to them and their interests. But big politics is about understanding our country and the people who live here, regardless of whether they agree with us or not. It's about getting to know people who are different from us, and being willing to listen and take into account their interests and values. We've been led into a trap. Our consultants may have brought us into this let's-get-to-fifty dead end, but it is now our responsibility to extricate ourselves by opening our minds, not only to the current instincts of our fellow citizens, but indeed to our own past. It's a big country. We need to get bigger in order to encompass it. "We are all Republicans [i.e., Democrats]; we are all Federalists," Jefferson said in his first inaugural address, after overturning the Federalist reign in the bitter contest of 1800.

The illusion that the problem of the fading Democratic working-class base amounts to a numbers problem of electoral politics. There is now an active and deadly serious Republican attempt to solidify a permanent alliance between big business and the white working class within the Grand Old Party. This attempt predates—and will survive—Donald

Trump's election and tenure in the White House. It will be no illusion for the Democrats if this Republican attempt to seal a working alliance between business and the working class should succeed—a conservative populism would prove devastating for us. Yet the problem could have even broader implications; it is more than a question of electoral viability. What's really at stake is our very nature, the very soul of the Democratic Party, and the ends to which we apply our power in the political struggle.

The illusion that we're powerless to do anything to get ourselves out of the mess we're in. This, of course, would be the final surrender, the saying of the last rites over the promise of American democracy, which we ourselves have done so much to expand for the last two and a quarter centuries. Defiance is the answer. Rank-and-file Democrats *are* the Democratic Party. They hold in their hands the raw power to change both the Democratic Party and the nation. They must reassert themselves now and take command, once again, of the Party of The People, and use it for the highest purposes of the Republic. Emphatically, it is possible.

How are we to do this?

THE POLITICS OF DEMOCRATIC MYTH

The master key to understanding our modern story is political myth. And there is a rule that goes with that key: *there is no politics without myth.*

Political myth is the gene that will recur throughout this book. A political myth is not an illusion and it's not a fantasy. It's the opposite. Indeed, political myth is the most powerful reality there is in politics. Political myth is the organizer of political thought. An ideal is a myth. A bedrock principle of political faith is a myth. In this sense, "The Party of The People" is a myth. Myths are big, simple, and ambiguous yet bluntly understandable. They are the fuel of our passion. They are what lie beneath all the rest. There is no meaning to political maneuver unless there is an understanding of the ultimate purposes that lie behind the political maneuver. *Myths are the purposes of politics.*

A political myth has the quality of both a beginning and an end. A political myth is the beginning because it's where you start your consideration of a problem of power or governance. You apply the philosophical lens first, before you do anything else. "All men are created equal." This is not sufficient, but it is the critical foundation. Of course, you look to the facts before you as well: this is the way myth gets translated into policy. To arrive at a practical governing approach, a political party must develop an appreciation for the new realities it faces, in light of the old wisdom it has accumulated.

A political myth is also the end, because it is where we are going, where we are headed. It is the ultimate goal and the purpose of our efforts. This is what lends myth its dynamic character. "The supremacy of the individual." It isn't true. But if you believe in it, you have to keep working at it, even as you understand that you will never cross the finish line, that you will never actually succeed in bringing the myth to fruition. But you can get closer.

The generality of a myth helps because everyone understands that there can be various ways to go about making the myth into reality. This is the difference between political myth and political ideology, and it is critical. Ideology is rigid, and demands fealty to every last jot and tittle in the details. This is why ideology is fundamentally un-American. By contrast, myth overarches all else, including governing methods. It is flexible, and invites discussion and experimentation, asking only serious progress toward an agreed-upon goal.

Democrats today need to apply an informing instinct to our political problems. Thomas Jefferson understood this crucial organizing principle from the beginning. In his great first inaugural address, at the head of his new political party, he plumbed the meaning of his election after thirteen years of Federalist rule. Immediately, he listed "the essential principles of our Government," because, he said, the People had a right to know, at the outset, what he deemed those principles to be, since he intended to apply them in the administration of the country. Those principles, he emphasized, "should be the creed of our political faith, the text of civic instruction, the touchstone by which to try the services of those we trust; and"—now the lesson for his descendants today—"should we wander from them in moments of error or of alarm, let us hasten to retrace our steps and to regain the road which alone leads to peace, liberty, and safety."

To ignore or discard this profound wisdom from the founder of the Democratic Party is to fashion a political shambles. In its feckless distraction, a political party obsessed with operational maneuver can simply get lost in the details, forgetting what is most important, forgetting why it is in business in the first place. That's when the Party has approached the moment of true danger: when it has forgotten or abandoned the things that might hold it together (its myths) and has replaced them with a preoccupation with the things that can tear it apart (the minutiae of details invested with an overweening supposed importance).

No two Democrats are ever going to buy into every strand of the Democratic myth in precisely the same way, with precisely the same fervor, and there is no need for that. But just as surely as there is not one political prescription that must be made mandatory for all Democrats—just as surely as the Party must encourage each individual Democrat to reach his or her own judgments in matters of political faith and fervor—nevertheless, there is, as a historical fact, an understandable body of Democratic ideals and principles that all Democrats must somehow come to terms with.

Democrats share seven political myths. They are our root ideas, our primal faiths, our organizing principles. And they are the building blocks for a new Democratic creed. Democrats must produce a politics of ideas before they can put into practice a politics of action. What we need first is to understand ourselves, so that we know where we want to be going before we start moving. So, first things first. We need to understand what the political myths and intellectual traditions of the Party actually are. We must look to the foundational and primal myths of the Democratic Party in order to restore our sense of ourselves and what we wish to achieve for America in this day and age. But how?

We can't just pull these most basic instincts of our politics out of thin air. They come from somewhere. They are in the fiber of the Democratic Party today because of actual struggles Democrats had with their opponents in the past over the meaning of the nation and its people. When those original struggles took place, they set up a conversation that continued down through the generations and exerted a critical influence over future Democrats, informing their instincts for how to approach the political problems of their own day. The key to the future rests in these past struggles.

Many of today's Democrats have forgotten these past struggles and the great political myths that came out of them. Without its founding myths, the Party wanders. There is a crisis of Democratic memory.

Yet even as we find the origins of our political myths in the past, we know that today's political conversation is and must be different from yesterday's. Therefore, when we look to the past, we need to do so with the firm recognition that we are dealing with the present and the future, not bygone eras. The future is our political problem, not the past.

Here is the master key that we need to turn in the lock of today's political stalemates. Today's Democrats are the bearers of a very specific intellectual tradition, of fabulous and fertile inner contradictions, of mighty ideals and profound, nation-shaping myths. This book is not so much about messaging or how we say things. It is about how we think. It is about the lens we use to view the world and our country and our fellow citizens. It is about why our lens got ground the way it did, and what that lens means for our struggles today. It is about *who we are, as Democrats*, and how we can prepare for the future.

We have all too often taken the easy way, and for too long a time.

Now, we must take the hard way.

The key to winning in politics lies in the ideals we carry in our hearts, and the ideas we carry in our minds.

We must search our hearts, and organize our minds, anew.

OUR TRUMAN—FOR TODAY

July 15, 1948: Harry S. Truman, accepting his nomination. We see him now in the old films, mounting the podium in the Philadelphia convention hall, dressed in a white linen suit. It is running on toward two o'clock in the morning. He is the man without a chance, deserted by Democrats on all sides. He is looking out on the humidity-soaked, bedraggled, and demoralized delegates on the floor. He doesn't even have a written-out speech in front of him. He fumbles with the microphones and there is a pause that seems to go on a little too long—and then the big smile comes, and, right off, he puts it to them: "I will win this election—*and make these Republicans like it!*"

The voters were tired of the Democrats after sixteen years in the White House. Truman took them on. The farm belt was fed up with the Democrats, but, he said, "Never in the world were the farmers of any republic or any kingdom or any other country as prosperous as the farmers of the United States; and if they don't do their duty by the Democratic Party, they are the most ungrateful people in the world." And labor—by then bitter and resentful of the Democrats—"labor never had but one friend in politics, and that is the Democratic Party and Franklin D. Roosevelt. And I say to labor what I have said to the farmers; they are the most ungrateful people in the world if they pass the Democratic Party by this year."

He demanded that the voters make a choice not between himself and Thomas Dewey, but rather between the Democrats and the Republicans. Truman reveled in his Democratic Party affiliation. There was an authentic, almost animalistic naturalness to his embrace of his party, and he made his foes seem natural to him as well. He made the Congress of the United States his plaything, the merest political prop. This was the Congress he had lost control of to the Republicans two years earlier—the godsent "Do-Nothing" Eightieth Congress—the whipping boy he made infamous in American political history, the one he said "stuck a pitchfork in the farmer's back."

Like every other Democrat, I love this story. I love it that everyone, including the Democrats, counted Truman out from the very beginning. I love it that he beat the odds and made all the smart alecks look like fools. I love his blunt, barnyard rhetoric. I love how he mortified the stuck-up and self-satisfied Republicans. And I love the picture of him the morning after the election, the one of him raising above his head that wonderful *Chicago Daily Tribune* headline: "Dewey Defeats Truman."

The '48 campaign is just about the greatest of our modern political hero sagas. And yet our retelling of it these days somehow misses the point, because it leaves out what is most useful to us Democrats for our own political conundrums of the present day. The significance of Harry Truman's magnificent 1948 presidential campaign for us now is not that he beat the odds. Instead, it's *how* he won. Truman's campaign remains today the baseline example of a lucid political mind practicing perfectly coherent Democratic politics amidst all the complexities of modern America.

That long-ago summer night when he accepted his party's nomination in Philadelphia, he told the delegates right off and flat out that he was going to win the election—"don't you forget that!"—but more to the point, he told them *why*. For instance: "The reason is that the people know that the Democratic Party is the people's party, and the Republican Party is the party of special interest, and it always has been and always will be."

He decided to make his argument about the ultimate ideals that lay behind and beneath the details of the controversies of the day. Truman explained the purpose behind the divide. Over and over, he hit it again and again: the Grand Old Party "favors the privileged few and not the common everyday man. Ever since its inception, that party has been under the control of special privilege."

The election that fall, he told the country, amounted to what all the other elections before it had amounted to. "In 1932, we were attacking the citadel of special privilege and greed. We were fighting to drive the money changers from the temple. Today, in 1948, we are now the defenders of the stronghold of democracy and of equal opportunity, the haven of the ordinary people of this land and not of the favored classes or the powerful few." The Democrats under the New Deal had brought great prosperity to the nation, but more than this, he said, "These benefits have been spread to all the people, because it's the business of the Democratic Party to see that the people get a fair share of these things." And taxes? "Everybody likes to have low taxes," but "when tax relief can be given, it ought to go to those who need it most, and not go to those who need it least." The "Republican rich man's tax bill" that the GOP-controlled Congress had just sent him "sticks the knife into the back of the poor."

In '48, Truman hammered away at smugness and privilege with a good-natured vengeance. The choice was The People versus the Special Interests. That's how he won. It was that simple. But Harry Truman was not the simpleton his detractors believed him to be. He was about as sophisticated and shrewd and tough as they come. He built his election victory that year on the big, simple, emotional foundation stones of the Democratic Party's most basic ideals—all our ideals, and not just the wellspring

Democratic myth of The People versus the Special Interests, or even the Democratic myth of FDR's New Deal.

All summer long and into the fall, he hurled these various Democratic political ideals into his dogfight with the Republicans. They were not necessarily ideals of the Democratic left; the left had bolted to Henry Wallace and the Progressives. They were not necessarily ideals of the Democratic right, either; the right had walked out and gone off with the Dixiecrats. They were not even so much myths of the moderate center. Instead, they were the ideals that the Democratic Party itself had created, and believed in, close to the bone.

And by the end of it all, Americans came to realize that this was how Harry Truman actually thought about their world. His world lens was the lens of political myth. This was how he organized his political mind and then set his strategy for governing the nation. Understanding this root truth, the citizenry brought him home, and his party with him. Harry Truman's strategic solution to the seemingly overwhelming political problems he faced was to merge the Democratic Party with its own political myths, outright and completely, and he went to the country on that basis. Not a single Democratic president or presidential nominee since 1948 has attempted such an absolute union.

Myth and Party—fused. There stood Truman. Our guy.

THE PARTY OF THE PEOPLE

Thomas Jefferson and the Individual

As Democrats, our faith is in The People. Here, The People rule. We stand with the many against the few. These are the meanings of our oldest ideal: the Party of The People. At the same time, our credo holds that in America, the individual comes first. We base our politics on individual interest, not special, or bloc, interest. The philosophical coherence of our coalition depends fundamentally on the primacy of the individual citizen's interests. This primal credo is what holds all of our constituencies and ideals together. In the beginning, we built our political party balanced between the twin pillars of service to the community of The People and service to the individual. This remains our political genetics today.

America had won its War of Independence. The Constitution had been put in place. Those who were in control—the Federalists— disdained the poisonous effects political faction would bring to

our national life. Then, an unexpected outside event would sud-
denly clarify the underlying divisions that existed here at home.
Force fields of basic ideas about the meaning of the United
States would align in opposition to each other.

THE FIGHT THE DEMOCRATIC PARTY
WAS BORN TO WAGE

For us, this outside event was the French Revolution. It was to
drive a white-hot carving blade through the history of America.
It divided the American people by instinct. This was the first
great forking off of American politics. It was to galvanize our
own political party and cast its fundamental purposes. Everyone
would understand the stakes, because everyone could understand the ideals that were at stake.

Who was to rule our country? Was a class of wealthy aristocrats to rule America? Or were The People to rule—the Common
Man? This was the fight the Democratic Party was born to wage.

In the summer of 1798, John Adams was president. There
was trouble in the Atlantic, and in particular with revolution-
ary France. Sporadically, hostilities at sea had begun, and
Adams, who was sympathetic to England, found himself facing
Federalist fever for full-scale war. Street fights were breaking out
across the country, with pro-war Federalists wearing the black
cockade in their hats, and their antiwar opponents, sympathetic
to France, wearing the red one. As all this was going on, Alexander Hamilton was leading a faction of High Federalists who
were determined to crush French-inspired sentiment for popular rule in America, once and for all. The specter of the French
Revolution provided Hamilton the perfect political foil: an

enemy abroad, with the blood-soaked mob loose in the streets of Paris, and an enemy at home, with the rising clamor of the populace for more democracy. He sensed that his moment was at hand, and he seized it. In the face of these supposed perils, what Hamilton demanded of the American people was "national unanimity."

The Federalist Congress imposed the idea of national unanimity on the country by passing the Alien and Sedition Acts that summer. These laws made it a crime to "write, print, utter, or publish" anything "scandalous or malicious" concerning the president or the Congress that might "bring them into contempt or disrepute." Prison could follow for anyone "opposing . . . any act of the President of the United States." A very wide avenue for the High Federalists, who plunged ahead by fining—and jailing—Jeffersonian newspaper editors.

Jefferson and his growing band of partisans saw these laws for what they were—not legitimate national-security measures, but a flagrant attempt to crush domestic dissent and bully every American citizen into fall-in-line, lockstep political obedience. Jefferson predicted that when tempers calmed, "this reign of witches" would pass, but in the meantime, resistance was called for.

It was the fight that forged our political faction, but it was more: it was a nation-defining moment. Here was the elemental struggle in the political pit that would begin to make real the promise of the First Amendment to the American Constitution. In effect, the Jefferson-Hamilton clash over the Alien and Sedition Acts was about power and who would have it: the already powerful or The People? Here Jefferson found bedrock in the rights of man. The sovereignty of The People. The sanctity of individual conscience. Freedom of the mind. Freedom of speech.

Freedom of political action. On this line of first human-rights principles, he would make his fight—not on some brittle states'-rights theory divorced from a larger purpose. He and his partisans appealed to national political opinion to turn back the autocratic spirit that lay behind the Alien and Sedition Acts.

At the start, it didn't seem to be working, as the Jeffersonian faction lost ground to the Federalists during the next congressional elections. Jefferson remained calm. In his mind, he could see the future of the Federalist Party begin to take shape, and it was a dead end.

Just so: the crude and willful imposition of the Alien and Sedition Acts marked the beginning of the Federalist finale. These grotesque laws were to bring them down, once and for all, when the citizenry realized, in time, the game that was afoot, and voted Thomas Jefferson into the presidency two years later, in 1800. He would put a stop to this slide toward elitist command in America.

JEFFERSONIAN DEMOCRATS: WITH THE PEOPLE— AND WITH THE INDIVIDUAL

The name for our party that I like best was the most common name in use for us during the nineteenth century. Unfortunately, this name is hardly ever used today. We were called, simply, "The Democracy." This was the battle flag we carried into national elections, and in the states we had names like The New York Democracy or The Democracy in Illinois. I like The Democracy because it seems to ignore the idea of faction and party. It implies legitimacy and permanence as well as the idea that if The Democracy is not in power at the moment, there is something amiss in the system, and the aberration is only temporary, awaiting correction.

The Democracy—there is dignity in it. It means something. It means *here, The People rule.* The People rule the nation and The People rule the government. In America, The People are sovereign. The People are meant to be in charge. As Democrats, this is our first political faith. The Democracy was a political coinage of the fiery Jacksonian Era, when our emotional commitment to rule by The People reached its zenith in American history. But its roots certainly run deeper, into the earliest days of the Republic, and particularly into the mind of Thomas Jefferson, whose words laid forth the liberal foundations for the subsequent expansion of the American people's powers and liberties.

Always, Jefferson understood, right from the start, there would be two parties in America: "those who fear and distrust the people, and wish to draw all powers from them into the hands of the higher classes," and "those who identify themselves with the people, have confidence in them, cherish and consider them as the most honest and safe" guardians of the public interest, even as he allowed that the People's judgments were not always infallible. Why, he asked in his primal clash with Alexander Hamilton, does it make more sense to place your trust, faith, and fate in the hands of a clique of rulers than in the hands of the entire citizenry in its combined wisdom? He saw the danger to America as emanating not so much from the many (the People) as from the few (the wealthy and the operators of the governmental bureaucratic apparatus). Jefferson chose the many over the few.

To Hamilton, however, such notional meanderings were juvenile and even dangerous. Hamilton believed in neither the individual nor the entire citizenry. Instead, he saw the legitimacy of the government as based in the power and prestige of the few: the moneyed and aristocratic classes. He didn't fear the few; on the contrary, he wanted to see their power aggrandized. Hamilton feared the many: the mass, the hive, the grubby and common sort of people. His every stratagem, therefore, was aimed at aligning the interests of the holders of political power with the holders of economic power. This was the kind of instinct that later caused Woodrow Wilson to remark, in a devastatingly acid aside, that while Alexander Hamilton may have been a very great man, he wasn't a very great American.

Hamilton's purpose was to effect a grand political deal: in return for the support of the entrenched, Hamilton offered permanent protection of property and position. This was the quiet political purpose that lay behind his great economic reforms of the Washington administration that established a national market in goods and finance: the funding of the national debt, making good on the paper held by the financiers of the day; the high tariff wall for nascent industrialists; the national bank funded with public tax revenue, put out at loan for private profit, for credit-hungry merchants. It was the first really big backroom political deal in American history. It worked. This faith in an alliance between the wealthy and the leaders of the government, so as to secure the legitimacy of the central authority, is bedrock to the political myth of the Federalists.

Jefferson founded a political party to oppose this Hamiltonian tendency: the Party of The People. Our party. This profound branching off would define the future of American politics and shape the mind-set of Jefferson's progeny.

Hamilton saw the State. Jefferson saw the Nation.

Thomas Jefferson was the first and foremost exponent of

the Common Man in American history, but it is critical to say right at the start that Jefferson did not see a common man who was mankind in the mass. Instead, Jefferson stood for the individual—the simple, separate person in all his reality and all his potential. To crippling ideas of class or blocs of people, our founder maintained a resolute hostility. Jefferson stood forthrightly at the side and in defense of the individual as Hamilton pleaded the special causes of class—the bloc of paper-dealing merchants in need of a bank, the bloc of landed aristocrats in need of a reserved-for-themselves legislative chamber, the bloc of industrialists in need of a tariff to protect their businesses. Hamilton's statecraft was built on class membership and bloc identity. Jefferson's statecraft was built on the individual as single citizen.

The supremacy of the individual's interests is not a right-wing idea. It is a Democratic Party ideal. Thomas Jefferson founded his political party—our political party—to uphold the sovereignty of individual conscience in America. We are the ones who introduced this political principle into the American conversation. We fought for this ideal over the bitter objections of our opponents. From the Democrats, therefore: the bedrock principle was the widest possible freedom for the private mind and the open action that might follow, out in the broad society. In this great ideal, which stands at the root of our national meaning, we found the key to our political dominance of the nation for the first six decades of the nineteenth century. These years were the high ascendancy of the Democratic Party in America, and even when we were kept from power after the Civil War, this ideal of ours still organized the political conversation of the nation and indeed perseveres unabated in the belief of millions of our fellow citizens to this day.

It is vital for Democrats to keep these two ideals in balance: the value of the big community of all the People together, who legitimize the Republic by asserting their sovereignty over the government, and the unbreakable dignity of the individual citizen, whose particular interest is the measure of whether the government is doing its job, and without whose trust the government cannot function effectively. The People, all together. The simple, separate person. Democrats must serve both these principles at the same time. Twinned, they formed our first purpose. The two ideals must be put together—today.

The trouble is that they are difficult to put together. They often seem opposed. Sometimes, as in the present time, Democratic politicians seem to insist on pitting these two principles against each other, highlighting their contradiction instead of trying to bridge it, and refusing to do the hard intellectual work of composing contradictory myths and ideals and making them compatible. Politicians like this have lost an understanding of the fundamental political psychology of the Democratic Party.

THE NORTHERN TOUR AND THE POLITICAL PSYCHOLOGY OF THE DEMOCRATIC PARTY

In May and June 1791, when Jefferson was secretary of state and Madison was his floor-leader lieutenant in the House of Representatives, the two men were in maneuver against Alexander Hamilton and his centralizing policies at Treasury. Jefferson was in George Washington's first cabinet, but in reality, he was moving into opposition. Things were not going his way. Jefferson was under pressure and experiencing very bad headaches as the advantage seemed to be sliding toward Hamilton and his faction. The secretary of state and the congressman needed a break—or so they said. Late that spring these two set off on a "northern tour" through New York, Vermont, and Connecticut. There were two purported goals for this "botanizing excursion" up north: to investigate the potential for a domestic maple-sugar industry to replace the slave-based cane trade with British island possessions in the Caribbean, and to survey the habits of the Hessian fly, a pest on the wheat crop. But though some controversy and mystery surrounds the purposes of their trip, it's likely that Jefferson and Madison were doing more than chasing butterflies. Clearly, they had politics on their minds.

New York and the New England states were unknown territory for the Virginians. The political cultures of these states were radically different from Virginia's. There was no acknowledged leading gentry in the Green Mountains of Vermont as there was in the sedate and settled Piedmont Virginia countryside where Jefferson and Madison lived. Control of the street was what galvanized the gritty politics of New York City. Connecticut, at the time, was probably the archest anti-Jeffersonian Federalist stronghold in the nation. Yet north went Jefferson and Madison, and they went because these places and people were so different from what they knew, not because they were similar.

They met for backroom meals with local anti-Hamilton political factions and newspaper editors along the way; with the leaders of the urban machine that had just seized control of New York City from Hamilton and his friends; in Vermont with the ardent Jeffersonian governor, who had just been elected to the Senate; and at the end of the trip with Philip Freneau, a college friend of Madison's, for the purpose of persuading him to establish the *National Gazette* at Philadelphia, which he did several months later, and which became the principal anti-Hamiltonian newspaper in the country. Soon talk started to surface of a tacit alliance between anti-Federalist politicians in New York and New England and the great planters of the South.

Democrats think of themselves these days as the party of government, as having the instinct to govern. It might be true, but we did not start out this way, and the way we started continues to inform the political psychology of our party even today. At base, we are a party of scrappers; we are intellectual scavengers and opportunists; irony is the principal hallmark of our tradition of ideas; disunity is perhaps the only constant of our long and storied history. In the beginning, we were not the party born to the task of governing; that was the Federalists, and they governed effectively for the first dozen years, with a clear and coherent idea of where they were going and what they were doing and who they were doing it for.

We, on the other hand, were a party born to the tasks of opposition. We jerry-rigged a ragtag and disjointed gaggle of partisans—you could almost say a party of leftovers—each with a different reason to oppose the Hamiltonian juggernaut. We were the Scots and Scotch-Irish immigrants moving, with a chip on their shoulder, out into the western reaches, away from the English on the established coast; we were the new and overlooked urban laborers; we were the small farmers and landholders so beloved of Jefferson; we were the great plantation owners of the South who had been outfoxed by Hamilton's dealers in financial paper; we were the creators of the urban machines; we were the pro-French. It made no sense at all. Yet this was how Jefferson set it up in the beginning, and by quite deliberate design.

From Jefferson on down, deep Democratic politics has never been just about getting more "people like us." Recovering the essence of our political party as a broad coalition of eclectic ideas requires reasserting a definite and specific kind of temperament. This is much more than a polite, momentary tolerance of differing self-interests and beliefs that might appear to run counter to our own. Indeed, the genuine Democratic temperament is in no way passive. Instead, it is politically aggressive. It demands a red-blooded and determined effort to seek out new ideas, and to sweep in more wide-flung views, not fewer. It respects ideas. It does not fear the clash of ideas; it embraces the thought that the clash itself can bring forth the best out of ideas that might seem at first to be poised in opposition to each other. This is the kind of party we need to rebuild in order to pursue the great self-rule goal of The Democracy. This is the temperament Democrats need as they think and act inside the Democratic Party today.

The lyrical Adlai Stevenson was the herald of the great post–World War II progressive resurgence within the Democratic Party. As governor of Illinois, he opened our national convention at Chicago in the summer of 1952. His speech electrified the delegates, who later that week named him the Party's standard-bearer. It was the last time in American history that a political party nominated someone for president who wasn't even running. This is what he told them in his welcoming address: "Here on the prairies of Illinois and the Middle West, we can see a long way in all directions. We look to east, to west, to north and south. Our commerce, our ideas, come and go in all directions. Here, there are no barriers, no defenses, to ideas and aspirations. We want none. We want no shackles on the mind or on the spirit, no rigid patterns of thought, no iron conformity. We want only the faith and conviction that triumph in a free and fair contest."

Here speaks the authentic Democratic character. We need to respond to our own intrinsic nature and behave like ourselves instead of like our opponents. What Stevenson understood was that while the fractiousness of the Democratic Party might seem like our immediate flaw, it nevertheless accounts for our resilience as a party. Governor Stevenson spoke for a broad party, a stormy, audacious, disorderly, imaginative party that would be governed by its hopes, not by its fears. The truth is that this kind of party is a strength to be capitalized upon, not a mortification to be hidden away. What is best for the Democratic Party is the very thing that so many of its current tidy-minded strategists, in misplaced embarrassment, do their best to cover up: the healthy push and pull of divergent instincts and mythologies inside the Party. Giving play to the underlying intellectual reality of the Party makes for more vivid—and successful—politics. It breeds a battled-out moderation that is well understood and instinctively accepted by the electorate. And, at the end of the day, it makes for better policy, too, because it rises from the ground up instead of being imposed from the top down.

If your first instinct is to get rid of people who are troublesome and don't agree with you, you are never required to get to know them, to really understand their lives and concerns, and therefore you can never search out how underlying connections of interest might tie them together with you. Entering into this internal Democratic debate means accepting the thought that no one has a monopoly on good ideas, and that we must learn to reconcile differences not just by finding the lowest common denominator, but by taking advantage of the vividness of strongly held opposing positions and embracing the best that is in them, even if they don't easily fit together. We've been able to accomplish this successfully throughout our history, but of late, we often seem to have lost this intrinsic touch that defines the essence of our party's temperament.

DEMOCRATS DRIFTING INTO DANGER

The Democrats have somehow seemed to change. The hold that the ideals of individual primacy and popular sovereignty have over us has seemed to diminish. The change began in earnest during the Depression. We had come to power as the party that had stood, first, for the individual, the party traditionally skeptical of grandiose schemes, the party of restraint. Yet we were the ones whom the nation called on to meet the emergency. To do that, we needed to show, right away, a sense of nationwide purpose. We did it. We adopted the big, cooperative measures that were necessary to save the country.

And, of course, the actions we had to take back then did change us. We adopted new ways of thinking about our country and its politics, and we live, uneasily, with them yet. The emergency was pretty much all-encompassing, and threatened the survival of the national community itself, and that's the way FDR and the Democrats had to deal with it and think about it in their minds. This meant the New Dealers started focusing on blocs of people, instead of one individual at a time: labor, not the man on the factory line; agriculture, not the tenant farmer; business, not the hardware-store owner; the Italians, not the Italian.

Yet after the economic emergency of the 1930s passed, Democratic thinkers, and significant numbers of the Democratic rank and file, citing the increasing complexity of modern society, still maintained this new conceptual focus on blocs of people, and less on individuals. Among other things, this apparent Democratic shift from the person to the bloc made it look like we had a diluted concern for individual initiative in society and the creation of the level playing fields that encourage it. We lost something we might have retained if we had been more thoughtful.

In any event, this has had major implications for us and how we are received by the American electorate. Have we now submerged the individual into the mass? There is a certain unfairness to this critique, but Democrats have yet to come to terms with how our point of view shifted, and whether this thinking in terms of blocs instead of individuals will ultimately prevail in our party.

Politically, Democratic bloc-think has become a problem. Implausibly, we can sometimes win elections even when we present the appearance of an intellectual shambles to the public. But the one thing that we will not be able to survive is the impression that the individual citizen has too often received of us lately, that he is being forgotten in our thinking, or that the result of our thinking is to pit him against his potential allies within the citizenry (indeed, within our own party). The individual citizen is saying to himself, "I am getting lost in the wash of great forces here; nobody is remembering about me personally because they are too intent on feeding the great blocs of their own political arrangements." And again: "It's a zero-sum game out there these days; if their bloc gets more, my bloc gets less, so I need to stick close to my buddies because it's me and my buddies against them and their buddies." The bloc-thinking of our political faction has thus become too much of a centrifugal, divisive force within our coalition today, not a cohering one.

But instead of deliberately tacking back to the individual, the Democrats began to make a virtue of the group—and their neglect of the individual—by plumping for a doctrine of "communitarianism," the implication being that groups were now more important than individuals in this country. Obama's oft-repeated campaign phrase from 2012 was "We're all in this together," and his inaugural address in January 2013 was largely a meditation on the virtues of collective action. "Stronger Together" was Hillary Clinton's mantra in 2016 as she built her partisan base of union members, blacks, browns, veterans, and women, bloc by special-interest bloc. Of course, ultimately we are all in this together, and of course we are stronger together— if there's a plausible public explanation of why we're stronger together. But constant and possibly gratuitous reminders from Democratic officialdom harping on the virtues of communitarianism came at the expense of the deep historical connections between the individual and the Democrats.

Are today's Republicans now the true Jeffersonians? And are the Democrats now the heirs of Hamilton? You hear these idle philosophical musings raised all the time among Democrats these days, as if a positive response is too obvious even to merit serious inquiry. But the short answer to these questions is no. It is vital to disenthrall ourselves from the bandied-about notion that the Republicans merit some sort of monopolistic hold on the cause of the individual citizen in our country's politics today, for the truth is that their crimped and one-sided interpretations of Jefferson's great myth of the primacy of the individual have often led to a constriction, not an expansion, of American individual freedoms.

Each of our two great political parties has always officially proclaimed its championship of the individual, but each party has a fundamentally different understanding of who that individual is. The key to this puzzle lies in the difference between Thomas Jefferson's laissez-faire and the laissez-faire of the Whigs and now the Republicans. The meaning of early Whiggish and modern Republican laissez-faire is grounded in a narrower conception of man and his strivings in society than is our own Democratic view. Our opponents see man more as a purely economic agent than we do. Their Enlightenment is more the English Enlightenment than the French. It is not quite a counting house view, but they see the unalienable rights as Locke's classic life, liberty, property, whereas Jefferson substituted, famously, the more gracious and fertile concept of the "the pursuit of happiness." It made a difference in where the two factions were heading.

Thus, we directed our laissez-faire toward the protection of the individual's free choice all across the board, in all the private decisions about his life and family, and we kept guard over his particular rights against the Whigs and the Republicans, who often embraced with alacrity a gaudy and extravagant politics that meddled in moral uplift.

To our opponents, man really amounted to a constricted, economic actor, pure and simple, so they directed their laissez-faire primarily into the economic sphere and focused it principally on the business activities of man. Therefore, the practical result of their brand of laissez-faire was to unchain the power of concentrated wealth by banning government interference with the actions of private business, or even focusing a too-close attention on the underlying rules of the marketplace. This is the key difference between us and our opponents—now as before.

The crystalline shorthand of Jefferson's original laissez-faire needs to be kept clearly in mind: the citizen's personal freedom is our territory; business license is Republican territory. Therefore, the Jeffersonianism of the Democrats did not descend into the savagery of the Grand Old Party's Social Darwinism. Instead, starting out as we did with a more complete view of

humans—more well-rounded, encompassing their many different concerns and pursuits and not just their beings as economic
actors—we fought our way through the GOP's Gilded Age and
into modern civil liberties, or what we called, more sturdily back
in the nineteenth century, "personal and home rights." The cause
of the individual is not, therefore, truly the Republican argument,
even if they attempt to cloak themselves today in the garments
we originally wove two hundred years ago. We, the Democrats,
are the ones who need to examine once again our roots, which
are different from the roots of the Republicans.

We are still the Party of The People today. We still stand for
the principle of popular rule. The problem is that we can seem
to stand more forthrightly for that principle when it serves our
immediate self-interest, and less forthrightly when it does not.
The primary way we Democrats now express our Jeffersonian
roots as the Party of The People is our persistent call for the
protection—and, indeed, expansion—of every citizen's right to
vote. This is honorable work on behalf of the American ideal,
especially at a time when the Grand Old Party, in tandem with its
allies in the judiciary, is feverishly at work trying to cut citizens'
access to the ballot.

But other Democratic policies and political maneuvers can
sometimes seem to call into question our first faith in ultimate
popular control over the government and its actions. Regrettably, we see this today, in a slew of headlines. President Obama
was wont to remark that "I've got a pen and I've got a phone," and
that he would use them to govern because of his frustration
with the elected representatives of The People in Congress. A
Democratic governor is said to contemplate declaring a "state of
emergency" in his state to effect a policy result his legislature
has explicitly voted to block. The governor's proposition is greeted

by boisterous cheers and silent go-alongism from Democratic partisans. We must take serious stock of ourselves and how we are acting in the public sphere these days. How do actions like these square with Jefferson's original imperative to oppose a political faction made up of "those who fear and distrust the people, and wish to draw all powers from them into the hands of the higher classes"?

The peril of our politics nowadays is that, with instincts and pronouncements like these, we are leaving ourselves open to the charge that we have dropped Jefferson's underlying political principle of popular authority altogether. Too many of our fellow citizens, including countless Democrats, are beginning to give up on American government today because they sense its actions are out of their control, or even beyond their influence. They're simply checking out. Solving this problem is critical for us, because it's a question of our own bedrock philosophy. The solution to public disengagement from politics in general, and our politics in particular, is not to withdraw more and more power from the hands of The People. Quite the opposite. The solution lies in the dictate of Jefferson's Party of The People, or, as Alexis de Tocqueville put it: "I maintain that the most powerful and perhaps the only means that we still possess of interesting men in the welfare of their country is to make them partakers in the government." We've drifted.

Thus, the preliminary and ground-settling task for present-day Democrats must be to find ways to re-establish the bonds of trust between ourselves and the citizenry. To do that, we must demonstrate to them with significant and substantive actions—today—that we will emphatically pursue the underlying political principles that Thomas Jefferson laid out for us in the beginning. Understand The People. Trust The People. Make the government accountable to The People. Put The People in control. Govern with, and through, The People. If we fail to meet this challenge, all of our other efforts will inevitably falter.

Every step away from The People has consequences. Even if the result of a command-decision policy maneuver, arrived at by executive edict, produces an immediate political advantage in the face of legislative obstructionism, the long-term effect is damaging to the legitimacy of the government and the Democratic Party both. This is the problem, and to be true to ourselves as the political progeny of Thomas Jefferson, we are the ones who need to admit it, and fix it.

In 2016, we lost control of the federal government, and began to operate in a political atmosphere strongly influenced by an American president with a pronounced authoritarian streak and the appetite for acting alone. Despite the drift of Democratic thinking away from popular sovereignty and individual supremacy, this is the new context in which the Democrats must now re-examine themselves and the modern meanings of their own creation myth as the Party of The People. Will the Democrats now rediscover their original zeal to trust The People and guard against overreach by cocksure central authority?

COHERENCE OUT OF DISUNITY

Yet to state that we are the Party of The People is to state a problem as much as it is to state a solution. If you decide to do what Jefferson and Madison were doing in 1791—deliberately bringing into the party new kinds of people who come from different intellectual traditions and follow potentially incompatible ideals, who come from different backgrounds and believe that they have distinct and possibly antagonistic interests—then you run the risk of intensifying the oldest problem there is in the Democratic Party: internal disunity. This is a real problem of substance as well as tactics, for if we are so divided among ourselves, how can we succeed in putting ourselves over in November in the first place? And if we do manage to get ourselves elected, how can we be trusted to govern coherently for the common good, when we can't even agree on what, in fact or philosophy, the common good is? We are always in danger of coming apart, and quite often we do. The Republicans have split only once, in 1912, but for Democrats, open factionalism is almost a parlor game: 1824, 1828, 1860, 1864, 1896, 1904, 1924, 1928, 1948, 1968, 1972. Everyone in the country knows this, the Democrats themselves most of all. So we need an answer that goes beneath the unity mantra delivered by party officials and candidates.

Democratic leadership has always tried to calm our unruly blocs of constituents by feeding them hyperdetailed campaign promises and as much taxpayer money as it can find, but today it often seems as if that is all we have to offer. Bedazzled by the technocratic expertise available out on today's hustings, the Democratic candidate mounts twenty different campaigns, each one puristically homing in on the hyperspecific interests of a very precise constituency bloc—Asian Americans in North Dakota who subscribe to a particular magazine, for example—and ignoring the idea that politics is ultimately a cooperative venture among lots of different kinds of Americans. Thus, our party nowadays looks too much like a grab bag of special interests competing shamelessly for money and power and another slice of pie.

There is no real effort to get the groups to talk with each other. There is no effort to do the hard work of finding an overarching philosophy that offers the different groups reasons to hang together with each other in coalition. There is, instead, a self-consciously intellectualized veneer of narrow policy-position papers that does little to mask a hollowed-out core that is missing basic, broad-based, understandable ideals and ideas.

In the absence of a wide conversation where different elements of the Party are pushing against each other, meshing ideas, and mediating ideals, a poisonous political dynamic can develop. The dangers are narrowness of views, rigid and willful thinking, intolerance of dissent, and stand-pattism: the musty whiff of refusal to adapt to new conditions. The danger is there today: such dissident Democratic voices as occasionally pop up to raise a question about officious and intrusive overregulation, or who put iron in their anger over the corrupting power of special interests within the Party's current-day cosmos— such voices are too often met with an embarrassed cold shoulder from the reigning orthodoxy, instead of an open-handed and fair-minded effort to understand where the other guy is coming from.

Under the fluttering banner of an ephemeral party unity, Democrats today too often seek to conjure up for the public a same-seeming smoothness. The result can feel artificial and even cloying to the Party itself, as well as to onlookers from the outside, because the very attempt is somehow an act against nature: our own nature. We miss the influence of rank-and-file Democrats in their vast and eclectic array—the influence of their independent thinking as well as their varied interests.

A political party is more than the people in it at any one moment. A political party is also a body of ideas and ideals through time. Ideas and ideals are also political realities, though they cannot be captured in a photograph. But there has been a tacit tamping down of thought inside the Party during the last several decades. As an intellectual proposition, the Democratic Party is narrower now, its interests and ideas less encompassing than they used to be. Today's Democrats are shying away from the diversity of their own originating ideals. The idea of the Democratic Party as a broad coalition of multiple ideals and interests that works hard to encompass its contradictions is not the cliché that it used to be taken for. Not anymore.

As a result of this narrowing down and tamping down of ideals and instincts, whole cohorts of our fellow countrymen who used to feel themselves tied inextricably to our cause, and, indeed, whole geographies, have left us—not only broad swaths of the moderate-to-conservative South, but also the rural Midwest heartland, and most of the interior West. The national party, in effect, is retreating into the security of its sophisticated coastal redoubts, with only a few islands scattered here and there through the middle. This is precisely what the electoral map produced by November 8, 2016, showed, with its horrifyingly solid mass of red running through the center of the country. But a national party needs to be truly national in scope, and the Democratic Party needs the geographies that we have quit, and, most particularly, we need the people we have left behind. We need them to get elected with, and to govern with, and we need them with us to raise the difficult questions that are always easier to avoid.

With fewer basic ideas around, and with fewer competing ideals that need to be brought together, Democrats run the peril of falling prey to the domination of one intellectual strand of their political ideals. Unlike the Grand Old Party, which can govern quite happily on behalf of a solitary interest, single-interest factional dominance is potentially lethal for the Democrats. We allowed something like that to happen to us twice during the nineteenth century: before the Civil War, when Southern slaveholders achieved a tacit veto power over party philosophy, paralyzing us into inaction as the nation slipped away, and again at the turn of the century, when the emotional storm of prairie populism seemed to eclipse some of the rest of the Party's traditional concerns.

If our party begins to recognize the untouchable doctrinal purity of a dominant ideal, it runs the risk of governing narrowly in service to the interests of that limited ideal. The temptation the dominant faction then faces is to govern for itself and by itself, and into the bargain it can arrogate to itself the job of interpreting the interests of its junior-partner factions within the coalition. Its overriding goal becomes putting its own policies into effect in their most correct form. But when its programs begin to falter because its base is too narrow to put them over legislatively, and its understanding of the country and indeed its own coalition begins to fail, the dominant faction must resort to expedient measures: the quick fix, the policy workaround, the decisive pen stroke of executive fiat.

It is at this point that the Democrats find themselves in potentially fatal opposition to their first and most primal political myth: popular sovereignty, the rule of The People. If they are to maintain fealty to popular rule as their guiding principle, Democrats need to understand their own past, and embrace the validity of widely divergent core ideals that they themselves first brought to the national political conversation. They need to search for practical and honorable applications of their own original fundamental principles, even when the strongest current echo of those principles might seem to be coming from their opponents. Our party's service to the ideal of rule by The People thus depends on a broadly based Democratic Party composed of varied and multiple political principles and ideals, as well as multiple interests. The way forward for Democrats is to embrace their own contradictions, not to seek to hide them.

So we need two things that seem to be difficult to put together. We need to recognize and develop the full panoply of the disparate core beliefs that emerge out of our own history and struggles. And we need a way to explain and resolve the consequent differences that could very well, and often have, split us apart.

A wide coalition party like ours is always in need of more coherence, if not actual unity. To solve this oldest of the Democratic Party's problems, we must again learn to think about our politics in a more fundamental way. We must make new sense out of older, larger ideas that hold out promise for tying the far-flung factions of the Party together with some semblance of dignity—today.

Thomas Jefferson's answer to our coherence problem? As Jefferson invented the Democratic Party, he enshrined the individual as the common intellectual skein that might bind up the Democrats' various ideals and interest groups of constituents.

When Thomas Jefferson put his mind to the purpose of his politics, the structure of his statecraft, and the chief end of the new government on this continent, this is what he wrote: "The care of human life and happiness . . . is the first and only legitimate object of good government." Hamilton he was not. It was the care of this individual citizen's life and happiness that Jefferson acted for when he held power in his hands. Jefferson's core faith: *The value of any particular action of the government is best measured by its value to the individual man or woman.* It's easy to state, but it demands courage and presence of mind to serve when the political deals are being cut. This part of Jefferson's philosophy is a standard that can be applied in any and all ages. The New Deal was a panoply of policies that wore a thousand different guises, entirely unconnected to each other except by one simple idea: that the standard by which a government program was to be conceived and had to be judged was its value to the individual American. The significant and difficult job the Democrats now face is to imagine for ourselves once more a politics that places the individual at the very center. With the New Deal, FDR's Democrats managed it in their day. We have not successfully managed it in our day.

Ultimately, the thing that binds the American Democrat to his fellow partisans, even at the furthest edges of our party's coalition, is a faith in the worth of the single American citizen. This means a determination to protect the dignity of the individual's right and ability to make the most important life choices for himself or herself. It insists on rooting the politics of our party, and our governance of the nation, in service to individual, not special or bloc, interests. A determined reassertion of this first faith leads the way toward renewed coherence for today's Democratic Party coalition.

WE MUST BE THE MODERN INTERPRETERS OF OUR OWN POLITICAL MYTH

Thomas Jefferson is the American statesman whose reputation has experienced the most pronounced swings during the course of our history: the highest peaks, the lowest troughs. This is probably because his public philosophy is the widest, and various partisans have latched on to parts of his writings to advance their own purposes, some of which have been lofty, and some

of which have been base. In addition, with the exclusive appli-
cation of cold logic to politics—always a mistake—there seems
to be a temptation to carry his philosophy to its extremes, landing him on the rocks of secession, or paralyzing him amidst the
shoals of an emotional and bitter opposition to all government.
He would have been appalled.

Twice during the story of our country, Jefferson's reputation
has plunged: during the Republican high ascendancy from 1865
to 1913—and today. A century and a half ago, his doctrines of
local control and states' rights were tagged as intellectual forebears of the secessionism that temporarily broke the country.
Less legitimately, given that the Civil War had settled the Union's
unassailable permanence, the reigning powers of the Gilded Age
likely recognized direct danger in Jefferson's fierce attacks on
plutocracy and entrenched privilege. "I have never observed
men's honesty to increase with their riches," Jefferson had observed. So the Grand Old Party demonized him and cast him
out for fifty years, before Wilson and FDR rescued him.

Today, the focus is on how Jefferson lived his personal life, and
the most forceful attacks on him come from his own party. The
apostle of American freedom was a slaveholder who refused to
free his slaves. The charge, in other words, is hypocrisy, and there
is no use trying to get around it: it's true. It is not only legitimate
but necessary to keep this historically accurate fact in the forefront of our minds as we consider his meaning.

But Americans have been drawing idealistic sustenance from
Thomas Jefferson for a long time. Abraham Lincoln, whose political party rose to combat the evil that was in Jefferson, began
as a narrow Whig devoted to banks and canals and Clay and
Webster, but as he matured into the greatness of his statesman-
ship, it was Jefferson he turned to again and again: a govern-

ment of the people, by the people, for the people is pure Jefferson. The greatest American political leader of the twentieth century, Franklin Roosevelt, is often thought of as the man who did the most to overturn Jefferson's doctrines of local control and de-centralization, yet FDR was probably his greatest modern devo-tee. Lyndon Johnson, on the night he gave the most stirring endorsement of racial justice and civil rights ever delivered by an American president, repaired first to Jefferson's "all men are created equal" as he sought to define the very purpose of our nation. William Jefferson Clinton began his presidency with a pilgrimage to Monticello. "Thomas Jefferson represents what's best in America," said Barack Obama, even as he pointedly rec-ognized that Jefferson's household was built and maintained by slaves.

With Jefferson, we must recognize and reject the evils of his personal life, even as we search out and make use of the good that is expressed in his public philosophy.

Today, the critical tie between the policies of the Democratic Party and the individual citizen is badly frayed and stands in need of clarification and restoration and re-emphasis. The Demo-crats need to restore their connection to this individual citizen. If the individual citizen doesn't maintain basic bonds of faith with the government, this is a major difficulty for us, as we are seen as the party of government, having built many of its structures, and having been at the operating switch in recent times. From time to time, however, government-aggrandizing Democrats are seen to ignore this problem, even to disrespect those who worry about it. We cannot restore ourselves as a party without restoring the individual's faith in government and his ability to exercise some reasonable control over what it does. The ultimate Democratic faith in Jefferson's supremacy of the

individual citizen is still the key to restoring the credibility of
our governance and politics.

By seeming to neglect Jefferson's public philosophy more and
more these days, Democrats have allowed Republicans to steal
from us Jefferson's faith in individual supremacy and pervert it
to their own ends, thereby gaining a critical and undeserved advantage for themselves in the struggle to determine the nation's
future. Today's Democrats have gratefully lapsed into a conspiracy of silence about Thomas Jefferson, our progenitor and the
fountainhead of American freedom. The way forward for the
Democrats now is to break this conspiracy of silence by defining anew the modern meanings of our originating creed.

"The earth belongs . . . to the living," Jefferson wrote. He also
wrote: "Laws and institutions must go hand in hand with the
progress of the human mind. As that becomes more developed,
more enlightened, as new discoveries are made, new truths dis-
closed, and manners and opinions change with the change of
circumstances, institutions must advance also, and keep pace
with the times." Even so, he kept his eye on the unbreakable core
that he had placed at the center of American politics. At the very
end of his life, he wrote: "Nothing then is unchangeable but the
inherent and unalienable rights of man."

When FDR went to Monticello on July 4, 1936, during the
Depression, to celebrate the 160th anniversary of the Declaration
of Independence, this is exactly how he talked about Thomas
Jefferson and his approach to statecraft:

> To him knowledge and ideal were fuel to be used to feed
> the fires of his own mind, not just wood to be left neatly
> piled in the woodbox. . . . He applied the culture of the
> past to the needs and the life of the America of his day.

His knowledge of history spurred him to inquire into the
reason and justice of laws, habits and institutions. His
passion for liberty led him to interpret and adapt them
in order to better the lot of mankind.

Thus, the lesson for our own moment in the life of the Republic: *We—and not the Republicans and not the Tea Party and
not Donald J. Trump—must be the interpreters of our own myth
for today.*

Therefore, for the Democrats: a renewed focus on the individual; a shift of emphasis to cast the tried-and-true in a new
light; an up-to-date meditation on the meaning of Jefferson for
today, in an era of active government. The idea that if we attempt
to restore, for our own time and in our own way, Jefferson's original standard for measuring the worth of government action—
that is, its benefit to the individual citizen—the idea that this
effort might be impossible in complicated times or somehow unworthy of us, this would amount to a phlegmatic politics of
clumsiness and timidity.

To focus our political mind on the individual American is
not to cast him off to fend for himself, awash in a sea of alien-
ation, and inevitably the prey of superior forces. A laser focus
on the individual citizen is not the path to chaos and disunity,
as some seem to suppose these days. The individual is not a
selfish and solitary being. The individual acts cooperatively in
communities of his own choice: at worship, at school, in sports,
in politics. Millions of Americans who are proud individualists
see larger purposes in their lives, and sacrifice for them. To insist on the primacy of the individual citizen in America does not
vitiate the need for an active and vigorous government to address
the broad and critical needs of society at large. If you focus your

politics more on the individual, after so long focusing mainly on blocs of people, it does not mean you are giving up on communities. What is called for, instead, is thinking these matters through at a more fundamental level, and a rebalancing of our more recent approaches, which have begun to stale our minds and stymie our political success.

The task of our politics should not be to manage the mass by dividing the citizenry up into discrete, stand-alone categories, feeding our many special-interest groups and lobbies, but rather to serve the individual and expand his liberties. If Democrats could demonstrate that purpose to the electorate, as a binding force for our very wide-flung coalition, we would find a readier embrace from our compatriots.

To be sure, no one can be entirely comfortable with Jefferson, and especially Democrats. For us, there is no one who is more difficult to embrace than Thomas Jefferson. But there is also no one who holds more promise.

2

THE FIGHT FOR THE OUTSIDER

Andrew Jackson and Economic Justice

The mission of the Democratic Party in the life of America is to help the outsider gain the national mainstream. The Party will bend its combined strength to the great purpose of establishing a roughly level playing field, smashing artificial or invidious obstacles, so that the outsider can have a reasonable shot at competing with the insider for the chance to get ahead. This is the political ideal of the Jacksonian Democracy. It must remain the Democratic purpose today. It is the path forward through the confusion of today's Democratic politics.

July 3, 1832: Martin Van Buren is returning home from his post in London, where he serves as the American minister to Great Britain. He is Andrew Jackson's closest political crony. Although it's midnight, and although Jackson lies sick on his bed, the matter is crucial and Van Buren goes directly to the White House. What Van Buren wants to know is what the president will do about the

bill Congress had sent him earlier that day to recharter the Second
Bank of the United States. On this matter, Jackson has kept silent
these many months. Of all Jackson's volcanic political clashes,
this is the one that will turn out to endure, and send an archetypal
political lesson down the decades of Democratic belief and
straight into this morning's newsfeed. Jackson's message is low
and flat: "The Bank, Mr. Van Buren, is trying to kill me," he con-
fides with a grimness not to be trifled with. "*But I will kill it.*"

HOW JACKSON KILLED THE BANK—AND WHAT IT
MEANS FOR US TODAY

Here stands the man in the field before the coiled snake, and he
has the hoe in his hand. This is the kind of winner-take-all duel
Jackson instinctively understood, because he had been fighting
them all his life. And now, at midnight, in the candlelit room,
began the biggest battle over the nature and role of private property in American society that the Democratic Party has ever
fought. Property: Who has it? How do they get it? What do they
use it for? These are the root questions Democrats have always—
always since Andrew Jackson—insisted on asking, and the asking of these questions has defined us as Democrats.

This was the great bank that Alexander Hamilton had
founded, and it was formidable. It held the nation's tax revenue
(interest-free). It issued most of the nation's banknotes. It had
the kind of powers that today's Federal Reserve holds. And yet
it operated like a private bank, the biggest private bank in the
country, by far. It took the citizens' tax payments and loaned
them out to corporations and individuals to garner interest for

its wealthy stockholders. Its affairs were controlled by a private board of directors. Thus, a private institution operating under a public license, making private profits virtually cost-free by loaning out the public's money. A sweet setup, in other words. So powerful was it that the reigning assumption of the day cast the Bank as politically invulnerable.

The Whigs and their forerunners were its champions, and Henry Clay, as he did so often in his long, alluring, shape-shifting political career, then running for president against Jackson, overcalculated disastrously in leading the fight to defend the Bank's privileges. He determined to force the issue of the Bank's recharter early in the election year of 1832, even though the Bank's license still had four years to run. Clay knew he had the votes in Congress to extend the Bank's mandate. He was confident that Jackson wouldn't risk vetoing a recharter bill for a bank that seemed so popular in so many well-connected corners. Clay had catastrophically misread the steel and nerve of General Andrew Jackson.

President Jackson came to believe that with the Bank, he had a "state within a state" problem on his hands. The Bank was so powerful, so private, and so unaccountable to the citizenry or to the government that it was virtually uncontrollable. During the spring of 1832, he watched quietly as the Bank marshaled its backers behind Clay's candidacy, and then he decided he would break the Bank, full stop.

He lost the first round to Henry Clay on Capitol Hill, but he vetoed the recharter legislation. The Senate once again passed the bill, in July 1832, but the margin was not sufficient to override Jackson's refusal to sign. Jackson's tart veto message told the nation why he chose to fight:

It is to be regretted that the rich and powerful too often bend the acts of government to their selfish purposes. Distinctions in society will always exist under every just government. Equality of talents, of education, or of wealth can not be produced by human institutions. In the full employment of the gifts of Heaven and the fruits of superior industry, economy, and virtue, every man is equally entitled to protection by law; but when the laws undertake to add to these natural and just advantages artificial distinctions, to grant titles, gratuities, and exclusive privileges, to make the rich richer and the potent more powerful, the humble members of society—the farmers, mechanics, and laborers—who have neither the time nor the means of securing like favors to themselves, have a right to complain of the injustice of their Government.

Jackson's veto ushered in one of the most venomous debates in American political history. The president went to the country that fall on the bank issue, posing it to the voters as The People versus the Aristocracy. He crushed Clay. So much for that. It was over.

Except that it wasn't over. The recharter fight in Congress and the November presidential balloting proved to be only the preliminary skirmishes of the amazing Bank War that followed. Every myth needs a dragon. Enter one Nicholas Biddle of Philadelphia, by way of Princeton University, president of the Second Bank: brilliant, handsome, accomplished, competent, effective. We should all be so lucky in our opponents. Biddle was to prove himself the perfect troglodyte. Yes, the recharter had been axed, but to Biddle this was but a temporary though irritating stumbling block. If the president and the Congress and the government and the People and the country as a whole had all failed in their duty to express confidence in the Bank's future, then the nation must be brought to heel and persuaded to remedy the error of its ways. After the Bank's extension effort failed, and its charter was withdrawn, the Jackson administration slowly began to withdraw federal tax revenue. This was Biddle's moment of truth, and he seized it. In a breathtakingly bold stroke, he retaliated.

Under the subterfuge of winding up the Bank's business, Biddle called in its loans, thus shrinking the national economy's outstanding credit drastically and suddenly, choking off normal business activity. It was a brutal display of raw financial power, designed to force the supposedly sovereign government to back down and grant Nicholas Biddle his new charter. Thus did Biddle artificially provoke an economic near-paralysis, the sharp crash of 1834. To the traumatized business community, reeling with the credit contraction masterminded from his office, Biddle would only respond that the Bank would not be "cajoled from its duty by any small driveling about relief to the country." One thing you have to say for Nicholas Biddle: he certainly didn't lack the courage of his convictions. Indeed, his strategy showed promise as the business community pleaded with Jackson to relent and accommodate the Bank. A standoff ensued. It lasted for fifteen months.

Characteristically, the president refused to back down. "Go to Nicholas Biddle," Old Hickory told the anguished business leaders who came before him in the Oval Office, begging for relief. "Biddle has all the money." Despite the nervous wailings all about him, Jackson understood that Biddle's actions were only proving the merits of the administration's contention that the Second Bank was an out-of-control state within a state, unaccountable to the nation's interests. And at the end of the day, as it was remarked at the time by the writer James Fennimore Cooper, hickory proved stronger than gold. Business and the country abandoned Biddle, leaving him exposed as one of the most audacious bullies in American history. General Jackson and his foot soldiers in the Democratic Party had prevailed in the Bank War.

In waging his titanic battle against Biddle and the Whigs, and in winning, finally, the Bank War, President Jackson handed down to us something so sturdy that it has endured perhaps longer than any other part of our political party's heritage. From his death-grapple with the Second Bank, Andrew Jackson was to grind a political lens so powerful that no Democrat, even today, try though he or she might, can truly or entirely lay it aside. At some level, all Democrats continue to interpret the world they see around them through the lens that Jackson made. Old Hickory's lens was bifocal: outsiders versus insiders.

Jackson's fight was for the outsider trying to get inside, and against the insider who would unfairly try to block him. Jackson acted to smash the cozy rules designed to reserve the bounty of the American continent and its economic potential for the well-off, well-connected insiders, and to open it all up, so that the outsider, the little guy, could grasp for it, could contribute to it, and then reap the rewards of his individual energy and efforts. Any venal or artificial obstacles to the Common Man's ability to advance his economic interests on a level playing field—these were fair game for the aggressive actions of Jacksonian Democrats.

OUR ECONOMIC LAISSEZ-FAIRE VS. THEIR
ECONOMIC LAISSEZ-FAIRE

Most Democrats nowadays should recognize their Jacksonian impulses in the Bank story from 1832, but the ear of the modern Democrat will sense that there is something off about it, too, something wrong, something that doesn't add up. President Jackson simply crushed the Second Bank and the coterie running it. One day they existed; the next day they didn't. Jackson didn't seem to approach his problem the way we might these days. He didn't provide direct help to the people who had been hurt by the Bank's dealings. He didn't even try to rein in the Bank, to regulate its affairs so that it would play a more benign role in society, giving the public interest an equal shake with private interests. This kind of program would be something that we might more easily understand today, the kind of approach that could lay the foundation for a long, logical, and philosophically coherent tradition in our party of regulating ominous actions by entrenched private business.

Yet the facts won't support such a story line. Jackson was a laissez-faire man; indeed, all Democrats of the time stood for laissez-faire, in economics as well as in the Jeffersonian sense of protecting private-life choices of individuals from government pressure. We were the ones who introduced the doctrine of laissez-faire to America. In economics, Jackson stood for the proposition of disengagement of government and business. That was Jackson's line of attack. He opposed the government assisting business; he opposed the government second-guessing and meddling with private property. He wanted divorce, not cohabitation. This will sound odd to modern Democratic sensibilities. How can you be hands-off, yet guard-dog the public interest at the same time? It is a genuine problem, and in order to address it, it is necessary to understand where the Democratic Party stood in relation to the whole idea of private property in the America of the nineteenth century.

We were not the worriers about communal rights and benefits, nor were we the proponents of regulating the affairs of private enterprise. We were not levelers. We were not redistributionists of wealth. However embarrassing it may be to some latter-day Democrats, we were not of the faction that believed in softening or cushioning the cruel effects that can arise from the operation of property within society. It was Whiggery, on the other side, that occasionally offered ideas for prettifying private property, albeit with marginal, cosmetic steps. We came from the opposite side. We were the party of private property, with an emphasis on *the*: *the* party of property, right up to and including a refusal to tamper with an assumed right of property in human beings, slavery remaining the cardinal sin of our past. Indeed, this is the fact that we must always remember about our political party in general, as well as about Jackson in particular—yes, we favored expansion of the suffrage in pre–Civil War America, but only to more classes of white men, not to African Americans or women; and yes, Jackson did speak for the outsider Common Man and he did threaten South Carolina with military force when it moved toward secession, yet there was also the Jackson of the Trail of Tears and the hundreds of slaves at his plantation, the Hermitage.

But in the commonly accepted universe of what was the citizenry of that time, the Democrats were radical egalitarians. When it came to property, we believed in a fair chance for anyone to grasp for wealth, free action for free enterprise, and unbridled scope for private property. Here stood our party.

Ironically, for a time in the nineteenth century, both political parties in the United States appeared to arrive in the same place: government letting business well enough alone. Yet modern Democrats are too apt to assume that the economic laissez-faire of our party and the economic laissez-faire of our opponents are both cut from the same cloth. This isn't true, even though it seems as if it should be. In the realm of business and money, the two laissez-faires were conceived for different reasons and aimed at different ends. And because the goals of the two economic laissez-faires were radically different, they produced radically different results. This is the point that is too often lost in contemporary considerations of laissez-faire.

The Jacksonians recognized the rights of private property almost without qualification. They recognized that the operations of private property would necessarily create distinctions of wealth. In and of itself, this was not a problem for them. What was a problem for them, and what they were determined to stamp out, was favoritism from the government. The Jacksonians believed that unhealthy perversions of the economic order arose from governmental favors. The gross anomalies in the economy, the theory ran, came from political cronyism. This is the whole foundation for the nineteenth-century economic laissez-faire of the Democratic Party. The Democrats were convinced, as a matter of philosophical principle, that no matter what you did, eventually the rich were always going to be able to enlist the aid of the government on behalf of their own selfish self-interest, and so the best solution was to keep the wealthy and the government apart. Evidence in favor of this proposition did not end in the 1830s—evidence abounds today—but as with any rule of life or politics that contains the word "always," maybe it was somewhat overdrawn.

Nevertheless, for our purposes at the moment, this Jacksonian idea explains why the economic laissez-faire of the Democrats was different from the economic laissez-faire of the Whigs and the Republicans. It sprang from a different source and impulse. The target of our laissez-faire was cronyism between the government and the wealthy. What Jackson attacked was an insider's game. Special, privileged access to the instruments for creating wealth was a fundamental unfairness in America. If the government was conspiring with the wealthy to pervert the rules of the economic game, that was an anathema. Was a man's wealth fairly acquired or unfairly acquired? Was he deploying it fairly or unfairly? What we have here is classic Democratic politics running down even to our own time. This is what the Bank recharter fight and the subsequent Bank War were all about. This is where our ideal of economic justice today comes from.

The game Jackson found was rigged. The government had been corrupted by the wealthy; the government was underwriting a racket for its powerful cronies. To put an end to such an un-American and antidemocratic monstrosity was a fight worth mounting, in Jackson's view. And despite Biddle's fanatic attempt to create an aura of invincibility for the Bank, it was still a creature of the state. It enjoyed a license to operate privately, and very profitably, but that license had been granted by the People through their representatives, the Congress. All Jackson did was withdraw that license when the time came, as was his right if he could find the votes, and as was appropriate, since the Bank was serving its own private interests and not the public interest.

Republicans today would like to convince the American people that the original core goal of laissez-faire was to preserve business unfettered and undefiled by corrupt governmental regulation and oversight. This Republican fable is a grotesque perversion of historical reality, although, in their own hands, in the plutocratic age of the Republican high ascendancy after the Civil War, this did become the meaning of laissez-faire, and it led directly to the cruel economic inequalities that the Grand Old Party masterminded, oversaw, and even celebrated during those years. Now they would like to assure us that this just-let-business-alone political philosophy is laissez-faire's only possible meaning even today, and deserves the imprimatur of the founders of the Democratic faith. The GOP tale is a travesty.

In the larger minds of men like Jefferson and Jackson, laissez-faire was no such thing. In fact, it was just the opposite. Jackson was trying to prevent the corruption of government—the weapon of The People—by private business, not the other way around. He was not trying to preserve business from any government supervision. He believed in the free exercise of private property, but at the same time he insisted on enforcing fair, transparent conditions for its acquisition, so that all might have an equal chance.

With a political negligence that is truly breathtaking, we Democrats today have been too quick to allow the Republicans to snatch from us the mantles of Jefferson and Jackson. The reason is that today's Democrats put the focus only on the techniques of Jefferson and Jackson—separation of government and business—rather than the underlying purpose or goal of their economic laissez-faire techniques. But it is the goals of Jeffersonian and Jacksonian laissez-faire that carry the prospect for a renewed and fertile conversation about the way forward. Democrats today should be concentrating their minds and message on the objectives of fairness that Jefferson and Jackson were trying to bring about, not on the details of their long-past policies.

THE INVENTION OF THE SELF-MADE MAN

This outsider/insider paradigm of the Jacksonian Democracy proved to be particularly strong political medicine. Our radical egalitarianism was strong enough to entrench us as the nation's dominant political party, with a consequent ability to set the terms of the national political conversation (that is, each individual citizen equal to any other, destruction of barriers to the outsider's chance for advancement, and unfettered fields of action for individual initiative).

Our opponents have seen all these matters in a very different light. For them, the essence of society has not been some universal equality in the philosophical sense, as it was for us, implying the right of every man to acquire and manage his private property as best and as freely as he might. If the Democratic faith ran to radical equality, the opposition's faith has always run in the opposite direction—not to equality, but to hierarchy.

In fact, their intellectual structure enshrines hierarchy. For them, everything is about distinctions between classes in society and individuals in the community. To the Whigs, it seemed only natural. There was a pecking order. Everyone had a recognized place somewhere in the hierarchy that was America, each person perched on a distinct rung of the ladder. The master and the slave, the teetotaler and the drunk, the man who spoke English at supper and the man who spoke Italian, the native-born and the immigrant, the man with a diploma in his pocket and the illiterate, the Protestant and the Catholic—they all fit in, but in different places, some nearer the top, some nearer the bottom.

Such differences were absurdities to Jacksonian Democrats, who saw no distinctions among citizens, but they were critically meaningful to the Federalists and the Whigs and ultimately to the Republicans. Their world was alive with hierarchy and precise distinctions of status. They knew it for a fact; they could see it all about them. And happily for the Whigs and now for the Republicans, the way forward in politics has been eased by a convergence of doctrine and self-interest. By no means was the object of the Whigs the eradication of hierarchical status. They, after all, were the ones who had the advantage by sitting atop the hierarchy. Democrats were more intent on smashing the structural barriers, and throughout our history, we have acted on that instinct. It is Andrew Jackson who stands at the head of this line of Democratic thought.

Our Whiggish opponents, saddled as they were with a mindset that saw only hierarchy because they themselves benefited from it, recognized that they had a big political problem on their hands, and they set about to deal with it. For once, they were serious. And so the Whigs constructed their own myth to compete with ours: the myth of the self-made man and economic opportunity. The Whigs sought to reassure their countrymen that there was enough flexibility in their beloved "American System" to offer hope to all, that they could move between the ranks of society and obtain new and better badges, more baubles. There was no need to break down the structural impediments to individual progress in society or the economy. This was America, after all. The individual could handle his own progress. Native ability and hard work were the tickets to move up the hierarchical ladder from one rung to the next. Here stands the famous self-made man. He is the invention of Henry Clay and the Whigs, and he is their bequest to the modern Republicans. You can see how this myth had everyday practical political implications for pre–Civil War America—as it does for today.

Rather than fiddle with real barriers to advancement, the

Whigs became practitioners of the politics of moral uplift. Our opponents were aware of the more benighted classes, and for them the Whigs would open a Sunday school, or the Republicans would shut down a bar. Churchly virtue would aid the benighted American. It would help him stop drinking. It would cleanse the slums. Sunday-closing laws, the sanctity of the marriage contract, English-only laws—our opponents have always been on the lookout for a new moral uplift that would confer more completely, more deservedly, the blessings of citizenship on the Common Man, or at least turn his gaze from other, more awkward matters.

With a sure instinct for all that was corny and catchy, the Whigs were deep into the politics of distraction. In all of American history, no one can match the Whigs as practitioners of the arts of political charm. "Tippecanoe and Tyler Too"—what could be better than this? In the meantime, behind their facade of flashy slogans and coonskin caps and barrels of hard cider, they were contriving to dish out to their privileged supporters political and financial favors, such as special licenses to build roads and canals—or, even better, the license to print money, which is what led them to blunder into the Bank War. Blessedly, they enjoyed but a brief life.

Of course, as time moved on in the nineteenth century, and economic complexity increased, and the concentration of wealth with it, it became more and more difficult to support the all-encompassing veracity of this myth of the self-made man. Economic problems grew bigger and more complicated, and Democrats began to come up with bigger and more complicated solutions to handle the new problems. As American society developed and American business evolved later in the nineteenth

century, Democrats and Republicans were indeed to exchange
their philosophies about the means they used to accomplish their
ends. But make no mistake about it. No matter the specific means
chosen, the Democratic Party stuck to its fundamental goals for
the country, the individual, and the economy: a fair crack at prosperity for the little guy who might not have inside connections—
with vigorous, active government increasingly the instrument the
Party used to accomplish its ends. And the Republican Party was
true to the goals of its own predecessors, the Federalists and the
Whigs, even as it changed its methods: the preservation of privilege and position was its overriding goal, and freedom from the
restraining hand of the People was its method.

You can get a good argument around the dinner table about
all this. The Jacksonian ideal of radical equality among all citizens versus the Whigs' supposed reality of hierarchy in society.
The Jacksonian demand for forceful action to level the economic
playing field versus the Whigs' hands-off myth of the self-made
man and his ability to seize economic opportunity on his own.
Jackson's myth—our myth—is serious, but then, so is Henry
Clay's. All of us, Democrats as well as Republicans, to some
extent believe this Whig myth of the self-made man, at some
level. Everyone knows examples of its reality in our country. The
point here is not to argue that our myth is better than theirs and
that we must maintain its superiority always and forever, to the
exclusion of the myth of economic opportunity in America.
Rather, highlighting this debate from the 1830s helps us understand who we are in politics today, why we feel the way we do
now, why we feel an imperative to take the initiative to remedy
economic injustices, and what our instinctive, steadying, originating frame of reference is.

THE INTELLECTUAL SPINE OF THE DEMOCRATIC
PARTY'S PURPOSE

It was Andrew Jackson who constructed the intellectual spine of the Democrats, who established the fundamental purpose of the Democratic Party, and his insider/outsider paradigm is the path forward through the frequent fuzzy-mindedness of today's Democratic politics. Here, in the political myth of the Jacksonian Democracy, is the stuff of social mission, something more than how to win an election. Here we deal in the currency of the essential function of the Democratic Party, and therefore our usefulness to the nation. Credo of the Democrats 175 years ago, credo today: the fight for the outsider must stand at the center of the Democratic Party's meaning for our own moment in the life of the nation.

The ideal of the Jacksonian Democracy remains today principally what it was on the first day: an argument about economic justice. The first Jeffersonian faith of the Democrats had been built on a well-founded fear of misdeeds by an overbearing government. By contrast, the Jacksonian faith was based on a fear of misdeeds by private business. It is really Jackson, therefore, rather than Jefferson, who provides the direct and precisely apposite response to Alexander Hamilton. Hamilton sought to cement the alliance between entrenched private wealth and public governmental power. Jackson sought to smash the very same alliance, as a threat to American freedom.

Beneath it all, Jackson's argument was about the Money Power, as he named it: Were you for the Money Power, or were you against it? No wonder he won his elections, and no wonder the election of 1832 was one of the most profound watersheds in all of our history. By imposing his mythological paradigm on

the national conversation, convincing voters to think about problems of politics and economics as a struggle between insiders
and outsiders, Jackson divided the American people and organized them coherently, sorting them into the Democratic camp
or over to the Whigs. The American Common Man knew, at
his core, that the Democratic Party was fighting for his interests. Furthermore, by deepening and intensifying the commitment of his party to popular sovereignty—persistently widening
the suffrage by knocking out property requirements, for instance,
opening it to more and more citizens—Jackson arranged to put
much more power into the hands of the People themselves, so
that they could fight for themselves. They understood what he
was doing when he called his party The Democracy. When it
was all over, the Whigs were gone. Thus did Jackson assure
the high ascendancy of the Democratic Party until the collapse
of the Union in 1861. What Jefferson started, Jackson clinched
for us.

Even though the thrust of the Jacksonian argument is intended as a direct appeal to those who get the short end of the
stick, there is no need for every Democrat today to become a
firebrand for overturning the entire economic order. The real
issue involves the search for balance within the parameters of the
Party's various and differing overall purposes. There is no need
for us to choose only the outsider's battles, to the absolute exclusion of the insider's interests. Such a politics would constitute an
absurdity in a country like ours. The politically aware insider of
means is astute enough to recognize that his own comfort and
position depend on persistent efforts to serve the interests of
those who are still trying to advance into the mainstream. Broad-
minded insiders will always form a legitimate part of our party's
vast coalition. Ultimately, Jackson makes an argument for social

stability by fighting to make sure all Americans—including those who still stand on the outside—have a practical chance for a dignified and secure place in this society, if they will work to make it. In the faith of Andrew Jackson, Democrats seized on a truth that is critical to the national well-being.

And Andrew Jackson's great goal of standing for the outsider retains a special place in the Democratic Party because it can encompass so many other strands of our national efforts. His broad purpose is the first principle we need to organize our overall contemporary political thinking. It is hard to conceive of trying to explain ourselves to the nation in the absence of Jackson's paradigm of the insider and the outsider.

The power of the Jacksonian principle inheres largely in its breadth and flexibility through time. It speaks to everyone, and everyone can understand it, and more than this, all Americans recognize that they or their families have at some point benefited from it directly. Intrinsically, it is highly individualistic because it helps the single Jeffersonian citizen, one at a time, and yet it is a rallying standard, too, for whole groups of people that the American mainstream, in its feverish distraction, has fecklessly ignored, or even willfully cast down. Thus, it sweeps up all kinds of outsiders pressing to enter and to contribute what they can, not just the economically disadvantaged. Outsiders of religious belief, of geography, of color, of occupation, of political doctrine, of sexual preference, of origin, of ethnicity, and of instinct who are by now on the inside have all advanced into the promise of America, thanks to this ideal and the fights the Democrats were prepared to make over it in the past.

The essential character of the American Democrat today lies in Andrew Jackson's battle for fairness for the outsider. Here beats the heart of our party.

2016: FURY—THE JACKSONIAN
OUTSIDERS EXPLODE

But the political heart of the Democratic Party has demonstrably aged and weakened over the course of recent decades. The political predicament we find ourselves in today did not burst forth suddenly on November 8, 2016. It has been developing and growing for half a century, and the last presidential election campaign provided ample warning signs to Democrats concerned for the survival of their faction as the country's vehicle for a civic politics of fairness, reform, and national renewal. It's checkup time.

In the beginning, this problem of ours was the handiwork of Richard Nixon and Ronald Reagan. Their weapons of choice were ideas. Addressing those working-class voters who remained loyal to the Democratic New Deal coalition, in a brilliant political sleight of hand they simply substituted one enemy for another. The plutocrats were not their enemy, they told the Jacksonian working class. Instead, their erstwhile allies were their real enemy: the highly educated intellectuals, the arrogant and self-serving elite that had grown out of touch with the country. This piece of legerdemain drove a devastating wedge straight through the middle of the Democratic alliance, which started hemorrhaging blue-collar votes by the millions. Essentially, Nixon and Reagan began the job of turning Andrew Jackson's political legacy on its head. Despite the Republicans' continuing service to the wealthy of the United States, Nixon and Reagan started to portray the Grand Old Party as the party of outsiders as well. The Democrats, in this telling of it, had become the party of the insider.

The Democrats have never mounted an effective answer—in

ideals, in ideas, or in actions—to the maneuver that Nixon and Reagan performed. It has become an ingrained, structural problem for the Democratic Party. It remains the most significant breach inside the Democratic Party today, a half-century on.

Blue-collar white voters overwhelmingly gave their loyalty to the Democrats during the New Deal. They were the heart of Roosevelt's grand coalition, which dominated the United States for over fifty years. Everything has now changed. Nationwide, Democrats have regularly lost white working-class voters in recent elections by margins of 20 percent and higher—an enormous percentage in politics—and in a bad year, like 2010, when the Democrats lost more seats in the House of Representatives than they had in seventy-five years, only a third of white voters without a college degree voted Democratic.

For more than a generation, essentially since President Johnson's Great Society efforts, the Democratic Party has too often simply ignored this political problem. In recent decades—certainly since the beginning of the Reagan era, in 1981—we Democrats have been faltering in our duty to serve the outsider. We have acquiesced too quickly to the political pressures of the day as the Republican Party bolstered the position of rich and powerful insiders, piling privilege upon privilege, stripping away the protections that FDR and his predecessors put in place to protect the chances of the Common Man. The Democratic Party has edged closer and closer to America's insider classes: insiders by virtue of their money or education or self-perpetuating advantages. The forever dissatisfied political party that for two hundred years had spoken most clearly for the interests of the churning outsiders in this country has now begun to feel more and more comfortable, with its outsider loyalists fading away, and its insiders trying to make do in an effort to win at the polls without Jacksonian blue-collar support. Democratic denialism is belied in the columns of voting results. Over and over, the story is told on election night—of late, we have been sweeping too many of the well-heeled precincts that used to bury us, and we have been getting crushed in too many hardscrabble precincts that used to constitute our staunchest strongholds.

The theory of the 2016 Republican campaign was to win the election by winning an overwhelming mandate from white working-class voters, and adding those numbers to its traditional support. It was a simple, exceptionally clear-minded strategy, and it worked. The sheer magnitude of Democratic losses among the white working class cohort in November 2016 was beyond shocking: the Republicans outpolled us by a margin of something like 39 percent. The generation-long, slow-motion mustering out of the once-dominant Democratic New Deal coalition became, in 2016, a full-bore rout, as working-class voters— mostly, but not only, white—headed pell-mell for the exits.

A political party that parades itself as the friend of the working man, or postures itself as the champion of the blue-collar American, simply cannot sustain itself in the face of facts like these. Democrats have an emperor's-clothes problem. This is the most striking hallmark of postwar politics in this country: the long-term dissolution of emotional Democratic loyalty to the interests of the broadly defined American working class. The long history of the Democratic Party in the life of America is marked time and again by high political ironies. Surely, this particular irony must rank near the top of the list, because it is so politically pigheaded and philosophically self-destructive for the Democrats, and because it is so unnecessary.

So how are we to approach this problem? Some in the Party

repair to big data. The country is changing demographically. Latinos are increasing, for instance, and whites are declining as a
percentage of the nation's population. This is true, and Democrats have been doing exceptionally well in Latino communities
recently. If 2016 was the election of the Rust Belt in the Upper
Middle West, Latino activists now tell you that 2020 will be the
election of the Brown Belt, with the Latino vote delivering Texas
and Arizona and Florida from the GOP to the Democrats. This
may or may not turn out to be true, and it should be noted that
the prognostication depends on the Democrats' ability to maintain an extraordinarily and unusually high percentage of this
particular vote. What is certainly true, however, is that this is not
where the country is today.

The American people made it crystal clear in November 2016
that without Jacksonian working-class outsiders, the numbers
don't add up for the Democrats anymore. There are not enough
Democrats to win a national election without the loyalty of our
longest-loyal constituency. This remains the abiding political and
electoral problem for the Democratic Party. Calculations about
how to cling, desperately, with fingers crossed, to "just enough" of
our traditional Jacksonian base in order to drag ourselves over
the finish line in November show no consideration either for the
Jacksonians or for the long-term viability of the Democratic
Party.

Can we recapture these voters? This is the great question of
broad, mainstream American politics for the near term: Who
will gain the loyalty of the Jacksonians, moving forward? What
will the Jacksonians do now? Will they remain with the Republicans? Will they form their own, third party to represent the
interests of working-class citizens, as a pure play? From time to
time, after taking office, President Trump seemed like he might

want to head his supporters in this direction. Or can the Democrats convince them to return home, to the party of Andrew Jackson—and the party of William Jennings Bryan and Woodrow Wilson, and of FDR and Harry Truman and LBJ? Can today's Democrats find the inner strength even to attempt a grand reconciliation with the values and interests of their historical core supporters?

In 2015, a determined insurgency took shape among the Democrats, seeking to wrest the Democratic Party's presidential nomination from its dominant faction. The dissidents were demanding that the party of Jackson return to its gritty originating purpose. This was the candidacy of Senator Bernie Sanders of Vermont. The Democratic impetus to help the outsider seemed to be rising again, finally, after long decades in eclipse.

The politics of the Democratic insurrection began to work because the American economy was not working well enough for broad expanses of the population. The problems the insurgency demanded be dealt with were real. Wealth distribution at the top of the economic ladder today looks like what it did a century back, during the Republican heyday of the 1920s, and we are headed for worse unless the trend is abruptly halted. These grotesque imbalances of money and position were plain for all to see, and not limited to the very poor, either.

Senator Sanders started to succeed. He brought young people to his banner. People could feel that he was in it for purposes that he honestly believed in. His populist rhetoric telegraphed his support for the working-class outsider. He was carrying critical states in the Upper Midwest, where some of the worst problems were to be found. He proved that there were white working-class Democrats who did want to come home again. His rough-and-ready candidacy was thus a step in the direction of Jacksonian purpose. But the insurgency, which burst with such force in 2015, crested and fell short in 2016.

The calling card of this Democratic revolt was income inequality. Unfortunately, there were some serious problems, both political and philosophical, with this Democratic argument about income inequality in America. Politically, the argument didn't work well enough, in the sense that it didn't effectively enough reach those it was designed to assist, and enlist. Sometimes the argument could seem awkward, even rigid and European, as its abstract rhetoric isolated the problem it cared most about, and failed to link it to other ideals and constituencies of the Democratic Party, such as civil rights.

Furthermore, when you talk about the evils of income inequality, you imply that you aim to equalize income somehow, but the truth is that the instinct to level outcomes class-wide across society falls decidedly outside the broad traditions of the Democratic Party's thinking. From the beginning, our focus has been on the single person and on individual actions, not on some supposed mass identification in economic class, as in "the top one percent." We have never framed the argument in ways like "Because you have it, we will take it away." Democrats can't credibly demand rough income equality in America, or anything approaching it. We don't have the money, or the will, and we would never get the political support for such a program anyway, from either insiders or outsiders.

Instead, the traditional Democratic focus in these matters has been directed squarely to the question of how a person acquired his wealth, and how he deployed it in society. If we discovered unfair or illegal methods of amassing wealth, there was our order of battle. Where we discovered a crooked system rigged in favor of the already privileged, there was our line of attack. This was why Andrew Jackson fell so voraciously on Nicholas Biddle. There has always been a critical linkage to our political strategy, a sine qua non for us, and that has been a tie between unfair action and wealth. Wealth itself, even gross inequality of wealth in society, has not been enough to bring us to full political battle stations. The Party has always responded no. We always stop short. We need the evidence of unclean hands before we unsheathe the sword.

No doubt some in our party will be disappointed by our refusal to charge whole hog into the class war. They might be frustrated by our need to discover the evidence of crime before we sound the bugle. They should take heart. There are bad actors all about. There is plenty of evidence of privilege taking unfair advantage. What is amazing is how many opportunities the Democrats passed up during the past decade to go after malefactors by prosecuting them under the law, and by turning up the political heat and rhetoric on evildoers, making of them personal examples of why the system needs to be reformed. Such attacks are not to be properly understood as mere personal vilification, because in truth it is the system, and not the politician, and not the crooked businessman himself, and not the class, that is the real target.

An economic system skewed to the interests of the already entrenched is what allows economic and income inequality to persist and even metastasize in our country. And when the system is out of whack, it is a public-spirited, idealistic, and even profoundly conservative instinct to try to fix the problem. It is fiendishly difficult to reform an entire system. It takes more than a good, well-reasoned argument. It takes more than facts and figures. A learned lecture in economic theory doesn't cut it. It requires a politics that is dramatically conceived and promulgated, so as to be memorable in the mind of the voter—and often this means a personalized politics to illustrate the point. Where is Mr. Biddle when we need him? This is the Jacksonian tradition at the heart of our party's purpose. And like the rest of the Jacksonian tradition, it requires political guts. But it works—if you use it.

The critical fact is that the faltered rebellion within the Democratic Party only highlights the truth that in 2016, the Jacksonians wrote their story not inside the traditional home that they had by and large deserted, but within the Republican Party instead. The fight in the Democratic Party was tepid compared with the raw emotions on display among our opponents. The Republicans were filled with fury. They set upon themselves, hammer and tongs. Sometimes they seemed to be slipping into the shadows of national life, but it was an honest fight, beneath the lurid rhetoric, between constituencies with differing aims and interests, holding different philosophies of government and following different ideals. The Democrats were palpably relieved. But in the story of 2016, Democrats should have recognized a larger political truth: long-term, the fact that the Jacksonians were doing battle within the Grand Old Party was ominous, perhaps even life-threatening, for the party of Jackson.

In the event, the standard-bearers of the Grand Old Party's establishment were decimated. The triumphalist outsiders seized the Republican banner.

And then they turned their wrath on the Democrats.

BEYOND MATH, INTO MEANING

Certainly, the Republicans now enjoy major advantages in this contest for Jacksonian loyalty. They hold the federal government, allowing them to produce the benefits Washington might bestow on the people who brought them to victory. They could, theoretically, govern their way to a permanent hold on working-class America's allegiance. But the underlying truth is that, although the Jacksonians captured the GOP nomination, and then saw that party through to victory in the fall, their position among our opponents was not clarified by the 2016 election. The Jacksonians would continue to be beset by the many Republican factions made uneasy by their presence. The rival internal factions of the Republican Party continue to pursue goals that are incompatible with each other. Thus, the November 2016 vote would not settle new political alliances in long-term stability. The Jacksonians constitute the biggest group of outsiders that is unrepresented in the country's politics today. The fight for their loyalty is only now beginning. It will shape the future of our country. It will define the essence of our own political party.

The Democratic fall campaign in 2016 did not offer much hope of a grand-design step forward. Sensing a toxic atmosphere, the Democrats seemed just to leave the Jacksonians alone as much as they could. Democratic strategists returned to their familiar home base: go back to square one; find only the tried-and-true kinds of people we're sure of; turn them out; leave it at that. It lost the election for us. The Democrats had taken the narrow view—of themselves, of the possibilities for their own coalition, and of the country. This was tactics politics, maneuvering back into a very dicey status quo, in search simply of more "people like us." It was the antithesis of the design of Jefferson and Madison on their foundational "northern tour," as they trained their great political minds and energies on constructing a broad coalition of the many to produce a government of the People.

And indeed, the reigning mind-set of the Democratic Party today has too often seemed to diverge from the way the traditional base constituency of the Party thinks. Democratic insiders and strategists and officeholders can too often come across as a much-knowing class of Americans who do not live the lives the Jacksonians do, and some of this Democratic chitchat and even public lingo is more than a little patronizing—the notion, for instance, that the working class has "misunderstood" its own "true" interests, that it has become embittered and distracted by guns and religion, and thereby winds up voting the "wrong" way. This kind of cringe-making loose talk is not only ignorant; it shows profound disrespect. This is meritocratic hubris on gaudy display, virtually taunting our compatriots to take retribution on us. It also misses the main point entirely, for it is the job of Democrats to understand the Jacksonians and give them good reason to enlist with us, and we have been failing at our job. Even worse, calculated smears of our opponents as "deplorables" who are "irredeemable" move way beyond the merely clumsy, and reveal far too much about basic instinct, amounting almost to political sacrilege for the candidate who had accepted the highest act of trust the Democratic Party could bestow in 2016.

Stories like these reveal a party in danger of losing a guiding overall philosophy for what it is doing, lacking the political imagination to step beyond momentary tactics into bedrock purpose. The damage done goes way beyond the electoral math. What is the meaning of the Jacksonian leave-taking? A political spiral spins within our party: Jacksonians abandoning the Democratic Party; less mention of Jacksonian justice for the Common Man; less support from the Common Man; fewer Jacksonian outsiders in the Party; less pressure on the Party to stand up for a fair shot for the outsider. And so on. No matter the sequencing of the reasons for this political power dive, the logic behind it is impeccable. The endgame is ominous. This spiral has changed our party, visibly and tangibly, as well as spiritually and intellectually. With ever fewer Jacksonians at the heart of the Party, our political purpose has become muddied.

Today, the Democratic Party does continue to stand, honorably, for the outsider in America—in fact, for many discrete groups of outsiders. Among its racially and ethnically defined coalition-building blocs it generally enjoys heavy majorities in the election returns. The lead the Democratic Party holds among these outsiders is strong indeed, and will remain so, if we remain true to ourselves. It makes sense for the Party to continue to stand for these Americans, as a practical electoral matter. And to stick close to the groups that have sustained us is more than a matter of electoral calculation for today's Democrats: it's a matter of political mission. The Democratic Party has accomplished mighty works for these groups of outsiders—in voting rights and civil rights, for instance—and in the process, we have strengthened our country by upholding its highest idealistic traditions. Yet the Jacksonian working class is one group of outsiders the Democratic Party seems to have lost the ability to reach.

Democrats must emphatically reject the proposition that there is some necessary contradiction between serving the interests of the Jacksonian working class and serving the interests of other outsiders for whom the Party honorably stands. Today, Democrats must champion the idea that the appeal to outsiders must embrace all outsiders, no matter their color or ethnicity or particular interests, because standing on the outside can create common values and social solidarity, if you think hard enough about it, and work hard enough to achieve it. This means that Democrats need to break down the walls that they have erected to separate off their groups of outsider supporters, one from another. We need to construct a public narrative of ideals that the Jacksonians can understand and lock into, and that can demonstrate the dignity and practical value of entering into alliances with other cohorts of Democrats. Throughout our history, this is the message we have delivered again and again, but recent election returns show that we have forgotten how to do that.

The best Democratic politics for today and into the immediate future is the same thing that is best for the country: determined service to the outsider. If the Democrats do not pursue the interests of hardworking outsiders straining to enter the mainstream, American society will calcify. Indeed, this is just what the studies are showing these days with alarming uniformity: our social mobility along the economic scale has largely halted; we now rank last among the world's industrial democracies in this category. To more and more Americans, the promise of upward economic mobility, as a remedy for the increasing inequalities of our society these days, seems like a hollow slogan. Therefore, a lot of what passes for conventional wisdom inside the Democratic Party today, with its delicate instinct to shy away from Jacksonian fairness for the little guy, looks more and more like the political strategy of past campaigns, not the coming ones. The biggest opportunity for our party could well rest in beginning to recapture those who feel most economically insecure, and 70 percent of them don't even vote. They've opted out entirely. But in order to make this work, Democrats have to learn again how to make an emotional and compelling case that we will stick up for the interests of those who are losing out in America, reliably and dependably. We could take the pessimistic and fearful view of our ability to reach our traditional supporters once again. Or we could take the self-confident view of ourselves and the optimistic view of our political party.

It's time for the Democrats to update Jackson's political prism of insiders and outsiders. We need to re-examine the underlying rules of the economic game that produced the imbalances we see in the America of today. The government set those rules. The political system can change them. Here speaks Andrew Jackson.

Trade pacts, globalization, internationalism, high-tech miracles for those who can operate them, efficient rules for those with money who want to move it anywhere in the world at the stroke of a key—the American economy that has evolved in the last quarter-century, largely under Democratic tutelage, has brought great benefits. But it has also decimated countless communities where Americans once gave our political party their almost unquestioned loyalty, in the belief that we would honor their deepest convictions about the United States of America and stick up for their tangible interests, perhaps especially when times got tough. We've let them down.

The kind of globalization that we endorsed has rewarded the rich and left too many ordinary Americans feeling left out and powerless to change their lot in life. No wonder millions of Americans, of all races and ethnicities, are feeling anxious and alone with their grievances. Today's Democratic Party, they believe, has simply moved on. In 2016, the national Democratic campaign provided no compelling responses to these legitimate and angry complaints, and sometimes it seemed as if the Democratic leadership not only did not know how to respond, but did not even wish to respond. This was a failure of massive and historical proportions—a failure of policy to be sure, but even more troubling and fundamental, a failure of philosophy and clear-eyed purpose.

Is this the Democratic Party we believe in now? Remembering their Jacksonian roots in the fight for the outsider, Democrats
like William Jennings Bryan didn't simply move on from the
small towns and debt-ridden farmers stretching across the Midwest and the South, and Roosevelt didn't move on from the
men in the breadlines during the Depression, and Johnson didn't
move on from the young men and women who faced the police
dogs in the South during their civil rights battles.

These leaders refused to be defeated; they refused to accept
the idea that nothing serious could be done. These Democrats
understood the profound Jacksonian purpose of the Democratic
Party's mission in America. They held fast to their own ethos.
They took the great Jacksonian myth of the Fight for the Outsider
and they updated it for their own day. They kept the stronghold
of Democratic purpose safe for their own party. They realized
that if Democrats didn't nurture and make their own myth
new and re-establish it for each new age, if they abandoned interest in the fundamental goal of their party, then they would leave
it to others, like Donald J. Trump, for instance, to put his own
personal brand on it. Indeed, as Democrats around the nation
began to remove the names of Jefferson and Jackson from their
annual fundraising dinners, President Trump chose Andrew
Jackson's portrait as the one he would hang behind his desk in
the Oval Office.

But Donald Trump's brand is not the Democrats' stamp.
Finding out what the great justices of Jackson's myth might
mean for today's politics is the task before the Democrats. We
must seek the good in Jackson—his determination to serve the
outsider, the little guy, the Common Man, his implacable will
to crush the rules that thwart the outsider's chance to get inside.
This is our own Andrew Jackson, the Jackson whom we can

make practical use of today—and not the Jackson of the Trail of Tears and the hundreds of slaves at the Hermitage.

This is the hard truth that now is impossible to escape: if we Democrats cannot demonstrate, through concrete struggle and action, as well as rhetoric, some steel in our spine in service to this, our own creed of helping the outsider, if we cannot show our own political reliability to the voter, then we should not be surprised if the voter does not show reliability in supporting us in our campaigns or our governments. The solution for us now is to express our sixth-sense political nature—and to act on it. We need to rededicate ourselves to serving Jackson's ideal and the people who stand to benefit by it.

From the Democrats, this job will require simply stated, blunt American idealism to guide the debate. It will require clear thinking and the tough, personal rhetoric of leaders like Andrew Jackson. It will require a renewal of honest mutual respect across the boundaries of traditional Democratic constituency groups. This is the hard work of politics, but it is the only way forward. Democrats need to face up to the reasons for the Jacksonian desertion, and treat it with the seriousness it demands. The Jacksonians need to teach today's Democratic Party—to teach it anew—about its own enduring root purposes in American life. The Jacksonians must make their way home, but for that to happen, the Democratic Party must first demonstrate to them once again that it deserves their respect and support—and that it can deliver the goods.

Therefore, if the departure of the Jacksonians from the fold of the Party of The People is the Democratic tragedy today, working intentionally and emphatically toward the return of those same Jacksonians represents the Democratic opportunity for tomorrow.

We have to think about what kind of party we want, and what we want our party to be doing for our country and for our fellow countrymen who all too often sense a narrowing down of America's promise these days. The Jacksonians have given a lot to this country, are contributing a lot to it today, and now a lot of them are in trouble, and they deserve the help of the great phalanx of the Democratic Party. The recovery of blue-collar America is necessary to restore the purpose and mission of the Democratic Party in American life. In order to speak forthrightly for the broad class of America's workers, the Democrats need first to think clearly about the fundamental problem, in the insider/outsider terms Andrew Jackson laid down for us. And then we need to act—and act decisively—on behalf of the Jacksonians, as well as our other groups of outside supporters. Full-force. Only then can we proceed beyond the electoral math to arrive at bedrock meaning. Only then can we begin to restore a sense of trust. For us, this is a lesson in soul.

3

THE POLITICS OF PENTECOST

William Jennings Bryan—the Social Gospel and Secular Altruism

God's work must truly be our own. Therefore, religion imposes ethical duties on the believer to act in the secular world: to lift the lowly, to succor the weak, to care for the outcast, to comfort the damned. This is the political myth of the Social Gospel, and our embrace of it just over a century ago marked the first great turning of the Democratic Party toward today's active secular altruism in the public sphere.

William Jennings Bryan was never supposed to have given the convention's keynote address. He got there on a fluke; someone more important than he was had a sore throat, and they needed a quick substitute. Twenty minutes later, he had changed American history. And, into the bargain, he had saved the Democratic Party, which stood, as of July 1896, at death's door. These things he accomplished with ideas. He tried to make it all sound like the old received wisdom of the Party, and in truth it was, but at the same time, he was changing everything. Those who today cast him as an anti-intellectual fool do not appreciate that he presided over—engineered, in fact—the greatest mind shift in the entire history of our party's intellectual tradition.

William Jennings Bryan was a politician of mighty purpose, and he needed to be. He found a debased republic that had been corrupted by plutocrats and their lackeys in government, all of them piously justifying their excesses with the most savage political myth ever introduced into American history. When the Democrats had no real answer, he was the one who stepped forward from out of nowhere to match the Republican myth with his own—a myth so strong that it echoes down into our own age and into the hearts of those very Democrats today who sometimes seem determined to misunderstand him the most. He made of it back then the reigning Democratic myth of his age, and he took it out into the country among the plain people he knew so well, and he spoke to them in their own words—he would not allow their voices to be silenced, and he would not be silenced—"speaking," as one poet wrote of him, "speaking like a siege gun."

And, by God, he could speak.

THE SPEECH THAT SAVED THE
DEMOCRATIC PARTY

Hear his voice as it rises above the legions upon legions in the Chicago convention hall—no microphone, naturally. In the old language, with the old words, he is explaining to the delegates the new meanings of who they are. He keeps calling the names of Jefferson and Jackson out of The Democracy's long past, but he is about to turn the entire political and economic philosophy of the Democratic Party on its head. The policies of yesterday are played out, he says, and he tells the audience that "changing conditions make new issues; that the principles upon which The Democracy rests are as everlasting as the hills, but that they must be applied to new conditions as they arise." Yet the question he asks about these new conditions is the old one: "Upon which side will the Democratic Party fight; upon the side of 'the idle holders of idle capital' or upon the side of 'the struggling masses'?" This, of course, is the most familiar question of all for red-blooded Democrats, speaking as it does to the bright Jacksonian line between insiders and outsiders. The economic system of the day has put the People's back to the wall, and now they will have to resist. "We do not come as aggressors. Our war is not a war of conquest; we are fighting in the defense of our homes, our families, and posterity. We have petitioned, and our peti-tions have been scorned; we have entreated, and our entreaties have been disregarded; we have begged, and they have mocked when our calamity came. We beg no longer; we entreat no more; we petition no more. We defy them!"

And now, hear them in their thousands, throughout the hall, from every side of the floor and up into the galleries, chanting it over and over and over again: "*We defy them! We defy them! We defy them!*" When the speech is over, with its renowned Cross of Gold climax, the most famous image in American political oratory, and he is sitting down, there is dead silence in the hall. Just the slightest, stunned pause. And then, suddenly, the bedlam breaks, the delegates stomping and weeping uncontrol-lably and throwing their hats in the air—and the cheering comes on and on as if to the farthest horizon of the farthest-flung prairies, lasting more than twice as long as the speech itself. The next day, the delegates would place their everything in him for the highest post. He is thirty-six, old enough to be president by barely a year.

There were immediate repercussions. The Populist Party, by careful design, had set its nominating convention to come after the Democrats' that summer. They had banked on the Democrats to put forward a presidential nominee from the establishment wing of the Party, thereby spinning out massive defections of midwestern and southern Democrats. The stunning and unforeseen nomination the Democrats produced exploded this well-schemed-out strategy, and two weeks later it was the Populists who abashedly endorsed the Democratic standard-bearer. And were never heard from again: it was the largest mass political suicide in American history. The immediate life-threatening peril to the Democratic Party was over. But there were much larger implications, too.

For the better part of the nation's first century, from the election of 1800 to the dissolution of the Republic in 1861, the Democratic Party had dominated the political life of the United States. The Party produced two leaders of the very first rank, Thomas Jefferson and Andrew Jackson, and then another, the grim and clear-eyed James Polk, who became one of the most effective presidents ever to sit in the White House. Along the way, the Democrats broke two major rivals, the Federalists by 1820 and the Whigs in 1854. The Democrats were able to accomplish this because they kept their eye on their purposes for being in politics.

The Democrats had seized on certain root American truths. They preached equality among all citizens, the supremacy of the individual, and fair access to economic opportunity for all citizens. These political goals were pursued by the Democrats tenaciously, even fanatically, and their strategy of individualism, radical equality, laissez-faire, and hostility toward insider cronyism was a partisan triumph of the first order. America and its people flourished, and they rewarded the Democrats, as well they should have.

Then, between 1860 and the end of the century, the Democrats passed through two near-death experiences. The first crisis was that, divided geographically, they were incapable of finding a solution for the terrible pressures that brought on the Civil War. In the aftermath of that conflict, because of their erstwhile southern stronghold, they were naturally stained with the stigma of secession. It is hard to imagine how a political party could survive dishonor so extreme, but implausibly, survive it they did and staggered on toward the end of the nineteenth century. Yet for today's Democrats, the second crisis is perhaps the more interesting. It was an intellectual crisis, the most significant ever faced by the Democratic Party in its long history.

During the second administration of the Democrat Grover Cleveland, the country experienced the worst economic depression of the century, the Panic of 1893, which sent the national unemployment rate into the high teens, and much higher in certain parts of the East and Upper Midwest. But as the crisis on the plains and in the cities mounted, Cleveland remained hands-off, with a crimped interpretation of the laissez-faire ideology he had inherited from Jefferson and Jackson. Not for the last time, the Democrats had made the mistake of endorsing a policy technique rather than a fundamental goal for their national politics.

So Cleveland was overwhelmed. He was overwhelmed politically because he was overwhelmed intellectually. This was the problem of the Democratic Party at the end of Cleveland's second term, as it convened in convention at Chicago in July 1896.

Its sitting president and its establishment wing had no way, conceptually, to think about solving the nation's problems. In effect, the Democratic Party was bankrupt of ideas. The country knew it—but, to its credit, the Party knew it, too. As the Democrats opened their convention that year, the delegates were presented with a boilerplate motion lauding the "honesty, economy, courage and fidelity of the present Democratic National Administration." They voted it down, 564 to 357. Anyone who has a taste for the necessary hypocrisies of politics will recognize such an event as extraordinary, but then the crisis itself was extraordinary. The man who resolved this crisis was William Jennings Bryan of Nebraska. How did he do it?

BRYAN SEES A NEW OUTSIDER

He began with a deep and instinctive understanding of the people on whose behalf he was to speak. It could well be argued that he was the most authentic of all the Democratic Party's heroes. He came occasionally to the small-town county seat where my mother grew up: Sycamore, out on the plains of Illinois. One day, the city fathers took him to the edge of town, to where the crops begin, just beyond the last house—to where, as they like to say in Sycamore, "you can hear the corn sing." There in a field they dug up a divot of the rich black prairie soil and put it into Bryan's hand, to show him their pride in it. There was a moment's pause; they waited. And then he turned to them and said: "It's so warm." They still tell that story in Sycamore, as if to show that he understood them and respected them and understood the place that had made them and that they had themselves made.

But right from the beginning, Bryan also realized that, if he was to fight back against the Republican plutocracy effectively, he was going to need to impose a new framework on the national debate. And to that end, he was to prove himself a master in myth. Shrewdly, instead of focusing on the Party's famous laissez-faire views of how the national government was meant to operate—this was where Cleveland and the establishment Democrats had got hung up—Bryan focused his attention first and foremost on the outsider he was trying to help, and on what this outsider needed. This critical decision opened the way for him—and for us.

Up until the great crossover election of 1896, the Democratic Party's thinking had really been dominated by Andrew Jackson's views of the outsider in America, and Jackson's views naturally reflected his own experience. Jackson was a hard man and sometimes even a cruel man, and he had lived a hard life across the mountains on the frontier in Tennessee. He understood his own people—the people he had led in the military, raced horses with, speculated against, farmed with, and even faced across the dueling field. He knew them to be resilient, tough, and determined. Jackson believed in these self-starting citizens, and they were the outsiders he fought for in politics. To fight for his outsiders, Jackson's concept was first to bust up the unfair economic rules that blocked their advance, then to get the government out of the way, and finally to stand back and let them forge forward on their own.

At the moment of Bryan's emergence, however, matters seemed to stand in a somewhat different light. The great economic trusts of the Gilded Age were metastasizing without any legal or moral checks, or so the evidence would seem to prove. Many, which is to say millions, were in the kind of trouble from which individual initiative alone would be unlikely to rescue them. This was because they suddenly found themselves facing a whole complicated, interlocking system that fit together like an economic jigsaw puzzle and conspired to keep the farmer down. The railroads overcharged him to bring his crop to market. The grain elevator companies overcharged him for storing it. Then there were the banks. The farmer had invested heavily in the incredible new machinery that was transforming agriculture, and the banks had loaned him the money to do it. The banks were calling the loans. Crop prices were taking a nosedive. And the money was hard, based only on scarce gold: the price of money itself was rising. Thus, the real cost of repaying the farmer's loans was going up. Bootstrapping alone was not going to solve these mercilessly combining problems. These families were in trouble. They needed help: active, immediate help all across the board for their numerous complicated problems.

These were the people William Jennings Bryan understood. He was to give them an explanation for their plight. He sent them a clear, blunt message that reached across the broad regions of the country—the far Midwest, just getting started, and the old South, searching for new ways to bond with the rest of the Union—thus throwing radically different political cultures into public alliance with each other.

As Bryan's outsider was different from Jackson's outsider, the politics of these two men were different, and their methods were diametrically opposed. Bryan's end purpose remained the same as Jackson's, but the way to fight for the new outsider, Bryan told the Democrats, was to put government actively behind the effort to solve the outsider's problems, not to leave him alone in his plight. Today, we associate this idea with FDR, but it was not our more recent leaders—not Wilson, and certainly not Franklin

Roosevelt—who first turned the fundamental political philosophy of the Democratic Party 180 degrees. It was Bryan.

William Jennings Bryan first implanted in the Democratic mind the idea that we were to become the party of government in America, that we would meet private power with public power, the active power of the state, in order to solve society's problems and make way for the little guy. And, as if on cue, following the Democrats' lead, the Republicans performed a political pas de deux: their rhetoric, if not always their actions, began to mimic some of the cast-off rhetoric from our old laissez-faire period. This is why the election of 1896 was a watershed event in the history of our country. This is why it deserves the name the "great crossover." In coming to accept the idea of ourselves as the party of government, we found a way out of our fatal intellectual conundrum and a way forward into the twentieth century.

And this is why Bryan stands at the center, not just of our chronological history, but of our whole modern purpose. He is, in fact, the pivotal figure for us. The pivot, in a scientific sense, literally. He oversaw the shift in our fundamental views of the proper uses of state power. Once that turning, which he championed, had been accomplished—once Bryan swung the hinge—we were then, and only then, able to imagine the great reforms of the twentieth century that we put in place and of which we can so justifiably be proud today.

BRYAN'S SOCIAL GOSPEL AND THE POLITICS OF PENTECOST

It is William Jennings Bryan's conceptual approach to the political debate, and not his policies or his rhetoric, that is most helpful to us for the quandaries of our own day. To understand Bryan's approach to politics, one must start with the problem he faced when he burst with such amazing force onto the national stage during the summer of 1896. Politically, the times were disgraceful, the most disgraceful of our country's entire history. America was a plutocracy, run by and for the rich. Its politics was sunk deep in moral and pecuniary corruption. The Gilded Age was the invented and patented creature of the Grand Old Party. Republicans set the boundaries of the political debate and established the common atmosphere. They won the elections. They raked in the cash. To operate successfully, the Republican Party needed an underlying philosophy, and it found one, tailor-made. Their political myth was Social Darwinism: the idea that social and economic forces in society should be left to play out naturally, and without interference, so that the strong might dominate the weak, thereby strengthening the entire community.

Bryan understood that when you were faced with an argument in myth in politics, you had to respond in myth. You could not do what the Democrats attempted to do in the 1980s: you could not sit and listen to Ronald Reagan talking about American strength and freedom, and respond only with the virtues of airline deregulation and putting schoolchildren in uniforms. Thus, as the Republicans had imported their theory from another realm—science—and adapted it to politics and economics in order to suit their purposes, so Bryan imported from his Protestant faith the religious theory known as the Social Gospel, and set it to work in the public discourse of the nation, to oppose the Social Darwinism of the Grand Old Party.

This is the rugged crux of the Social Gospel: God's work must truly be our own, and therefore religion imposes ethical duties on the believer to act in the secular world: to lift the lowly, to succor the weak, to care for the outcast, to comfort the damned. And here—in the very things about Bryan that embarrass so many Democrats today—we can find not a problem for the Democratic Party, as might appear at first glance, but rather a solution. The Social Gospel offers a key to the way forward, as indeed Bryan was able to offer his fellow citizens in his great crusades of a century back.

In the revival speeches he was famous for making under the Chautauqua tents and out on the campaign trail, Bryan liked to explain it this way. We have a garden, with roses and weeds. The weeds are stronger than the roses and naturally begin to crowd them out. Bryan asked: Must we stand idly by and watch it all happen, or should we take up the hoe and help preserve the good? What is our duty to society? Indeed, what is our duty to God? Bryan understood the people he was talking to. Instinctively, they understood him. They were reassured. No be-jargoned abracadabra of abstract theories like foreign socialism, from across the ocean. Instead, the Good Book; the old words. The most vivid metaphor in all of American political history, a cross of gold, was a direct attack on secular financial evil using religious language. Through the language of the Social Gospel, Bryan attacked injustice in American society and produced an amazing emotional response, a sort of Politics of Pentecost—the descending from above of a fervent spirit of truth and mission upon the people, an enkindling of the spirit of justice for the secular world. The Social Gospel moved the hearts of Bryan's compatriots, and did so honorably, and they fell in behind him by the millions, in the cause of secular reform.

In expressing sentiments such as these, using this kind of language, William Jennings Bryan was directly tapping into the same power source that has driven almost all the great reform movements of American history. The heritage of the Democratic Party is not so purely nonreligious as might be convenient for the secular stalwart of today to maintain. The period we have been living through recently is unusual for us. In fact, one can point to many struggles and eras when our party was quite closely associated with religious militancy. Even today's skeptics are not likely to rebel at these historical precedents. Many northern Democrats were abolitionists before the Civil War, and morally expressed abolitionism was rooted in radical reform Protestantism. American missionaries working abroad in the nineteenth and early twentieth centuries were largely responsible for successfully insisting that U.S. foreign policy foster free expression and free elections overseas. Hardscrabble Protestants were frequently allied with Bryanite elements of the Democratic Party because our economic program benefited those who were disadvantaged by the enterprise system of the day. Child-labor reform and the modern-day civil rights movement, to cite more examples, were deeply rooted in the church. Not to understand this point is to misunderstand our traditions as a people. To turn away those Democrats who wish to claim religion as their motive for joining with our party, to miss religion as an important moving force in today's America—as a fuel for secular reform— is to cripple one's access to the very people one seeks to serve.

Bryan wasn't the sophisticated politician of today, with all the facts and figures and policy-perfect arguments, secret pollsters, staff assistance, and economic theories close at hand. In fact, truth be told, economics was probably not Bryan's strong suit. Out on the Chautauqua circuit, he used to give a famous lecture he called "The Value of an Ideal." People flocked to hear this lecture in the millions. The story of his lecture is instruc-

tive because it explains his approach to the secular power struggle in the political pit, and it sets off his approach from ours
today.

Bryan's concept was this: he would go to fundamentals first.
He knew the bedrock basic human principles he believed
in—the big picture of where he wanted to go. He knew, for
instance, that he wanted to help those who had been crushed
and cast aside. He would state the large principle first, right up
front. Then, he would try to persuade his audience to his way of
thinking. He wanted them to move toward the ideal he had
stated. He realized he might lose the argument, but he would
make his case, come what may, and on this, in particular, he
would insist: he would impose his own framework on the debate;
he would demand that the audience, and the country, grapple
with the broad principle he was enunciating. This was the "value
of an ideal." It helped people understand their world and it
brought them to him.

At its most fundamental, in his three campaigns for
president—in 1896, 1900, and 1908—Bryan's public approach
was to make the moral point. We should help these people
because it's the right thing to do, he said, and sometimes he
said that we should do it because it's our Christian duty to do
it. Bryan actually believed that all of politics comes down to
questions of morality. As a sweeping assertion, this may carry
the point too far, but people do crave meaning and perspective
and something higher to believe in from the common public
discussion. A commonly understood morality can impart meaning to the political debate. In politics, relentlessly detailed how-
to lectures couched in technocratic jargon really amount to an
antipolitics. Bryan therefore stands at the polar opposite of a
lot of the strategic thinking inside our party these days, and

Democrats today could well take a lesson from the warm and humane sensibilities of the man who led our party as America was coming of age.

CHARLOTTE, NORTH CAROLINA:
SEPTEMBER 5, 2012

Since the 1960s, a lot of animosity has developed between ourselves and evangelical Christians who identify themselves with our opponents. It's been very tough on everyone: tough on us, tough on them. Both sides have deliberately dished out a lot of political pain. During the past generation in particular, we have found ourselves on the receiving end of a decades-long onslaught of public religiosity from our Republican opponents, and we've been paying a big political price for it, because the subjects of these attacks are often what is known in politics as "threshold issues." The historical record of the recent era would suggest that often, if you stumble on a threshold issue, like abortion or the definition of marriage, you have big trouble getting through to evangelicals on any other issue afterward. Some of these attacks have been quite cynically devised in a clear-eyed search for tactical political advantage, but a lot of the attacks are homegrown, and fairly so, too, because they represent fundamental differences of belief over questions of irreducible morality and doctrine. This is a serious debate that could have benefited from a lot more mutual respect from everyone concerned.

The improbable result has been that Democrats have been bludgeoned into official silence when God comes up, which has only made matters worse. On September 5, 2012, the Democratic Party met in convention at Charlotte, North Carolina, to consider the platform it would put before the electorate in the fall campaign. According to President Obama, the Platform Committee's initial drafters had made a mistake: they had written God out of the platform, and he wanted God put back in (a reference to each citizen's "God-given potential"). So the change was made and it was put to the assembled delegates for a voice vote and it duly passed, "in the opinion of the Chair" at the podium. But the opinion of the Chair was wrong. The motion had, in reality, failed to muster the required majority of the votes. The delegates, who actually had the power to express the will and official position of the Democratic Party at that particular moment, didn't want God mentioned at all. The scene on the floor of the convention was momentary confusion, and understandably so, but the real confusion was in the mind of the Party itself, which was perhaps less understandable.

Hearing the silence reverberating from the Democratic camp, the public at large has sensed the whiff of being above it all, an icy hauteur that seems to disdain religious faith itself and the manifold contributions it has made to the life of this country. Silence is interpreted as somehow implying disapproval, and thus our reputation today, among far too many of our fellow citizens, is one of hostility to religion. But silence and a refusal to do combat in the public square are not our tradition. And neither is a refusal to recognize the merits of religious faith. Jefferson himself would have found such a notion bizarre. For the citizen who stands in our tradition, the real questions are how spiritual values affect political judgment, and how faith fits in with freedom. These are important questions, and they can be difficult questions to deal with, which is one of the reasons Democrats have tried to avoid them in recent years. We have tried to avoid these questions by keeping silent about them. It hasn't worked.

We are never going to make headway in this discussion if we cede the terms of it to our opponents, either in frozen silence or in feuding over such demands as they may decide to make on us at any particular moment. Like the Federalists and Whigs before them, the Republicans will always outbid us if it becomes an arms race over enforcing restrictions on private personal behavior or plumping for moral uplift. To take up a challenge like that would put us on a path toward the land of the goody-goody or the land of the bully, in either case an unhappy terminus for the party of Thomas Jefferson.

The figure in our history most associated with a strong public religiosity is, of course, William Jennings Bryan. Bryan's true emotional and intellectual interests did not come to rest in the realm of individual lifestyles, however. His public career, while he flourished in the political life of the nation, really had precious little to do with personal behavior: private sleeping arrangements, dancing predilections, even drinking habits (Bryan, in fact, began his career as a lawyer for saloonkeeps). To read his Chautauqua addresses is to understand his gentle, humane, tolerant approach to questions surrounding private morality and personal salvation. Rather, the public arena was what motivated William Jennings Bryan. The Social Gospel was about the individual's duty to act in the public sphere, not about what the individual did in private. The authentic and useful intellectual tradition of the Democrats is to protect the sanctity of individual action in the private sphere, with a due respect and regard to what Bryan would have called the "personal and home rights," while engaging full-throttle in the public sphere.

When Bryan burst on the scene in 1896 and imposed the biblical Social Gospel on the secular debate, it marked the beginnings of a critical change in the thinking of the Democratic Party—one having nothing to do with the Republicans, and one that permeates the politics of Democrats today. It was the Social Gospel that first imparted an altruistic cast to the Democrats' politics. This isn't to say that there were no altruistic Democrats of good heart and intentions during the first half of the Party's life. Yet the Democratic Party was incontestably different after Bryan preached the Social Gospel. His language of morality infused itself into the spirit of his political party and began to exert a pronounced influence, not only on his own generation but on all the generations of Democrats that have followed him. Countless voters today, both religious and non-religious, feel the same humane and altruistic urges in the face of so much trouble and so many crushed hopes in society. When they come to choose between the two great national political parties, they recognize these impulses woven through the fabric of the Democrats' coalition, and not so much in the other faction. They feel more comfortable with us. These voters are people of conscience, and they are the political progeny of the man who led our party just over a hundred years ago.

William Jennings Bryan is the historical source of our instinctive predilection toward political altruism. And as such, he is the intellectual forefather not only of today's religious Democrats, but also of today's secular humanist Democrats, so honorably committed to the spirit of altruism for working out the terrible problems of America today, yet at the same time so uneasy with talk of religion in the public square. All of these Democrats, together, are, in fact, lineal descendants of the intellectual line introduced into our political DNA by William Jennings Bryan.

EVANGELICAL DEMOCRATS AND SECULAR
ALTRUISTS TODAY

And now, for the first time since the 1970s, Democrats might have the chance to return honorably to the evangelical constituencies that supported the Democrats so fervently in the past because they and the Democratic Party made common cause over common interests. There is a new conversation among evangelicals these days that reaches beyond the old verities of the marriage contract or abortion. There is a growing unease toward allowing only one or two issues to dictate political allegiance. There is a widening of interest in new fields for God's work in the world, and therefore for the work of His followers. These new conversations are being driven by a generational shift toward younger evangelicals. Many of the young in the community have a new intellectual curiosity and a new determination to join the work of society across the whole spectrum of problems, just as their individual hearts and interests might guide them. Human rights abroad and at home, family life, stewardship of the environment, the ethical content of education in the schools, poverty, foreign policy, flourishing neighborhoods, truth telling in the public square—the list goes on and on. Comprehensive reform of the nation's immigration laws, in particular, has attracted the special interest of the evangelical community because so many of its members are touched by this particular problem. These are all areas where citizens who are Democrats because of their underlying religious convictions have lots to contribute to the political struggles both inside our party and with our opponents.

Yet many Democrats who aren't paying attention still maintain the view that American evangelical voters constitute a monolithic and unbreakable political force in the life of the nation that cannot be reasoned with or successfully penetrated because it axiomatically turns its votes on a rigid and narrow set of doctrinal criteria. This view is false. In 2016, Donald Trump—who was historically and politically a stranger to this community, whose personal temperament and behavior did not demonstrate high standards of moral rectitude, and who often seemed to disdain many of the lifestyle social-issue causes that have hallmarked the platforms of our opponents during the past generation, in deference to evangelical belief—early on obtained the allegiance of a plurality of white evangelical voters and kept it, winding up with a greater majority of their votes than any of the three previous GOP presidential nominees.

Democrats today carry significant majorities of evangelical voters who come out of nonwhite communities; it is among white evangelicals that we seem to stumble so badly, and nearly 30 percent of all white voters identify themselves as evangelicals. It makes no sense for a national partisan coalition to ignore a political reality that looms this large. The numbers here are huge, and we have virtually ceded them to our opponents. It behooves Democrats, and particularly those secular Democrats who dominate our party today, to figure out how to speak honestly and honorably to their fellow citizens who come from traditions like these.

This is not to suggest, of course, that the nonreligious should trick themselves out as believers. The nonbeliever parading as a believer is a charlatan waiting to be unmasked. There is no need for a ruse like this. There is plenty of honor in being either a Democrat as nonbeliever or a Democrat from religious conviction. Democrats in the past, including Bryan, have successfully used economic arguments, and the full range of our other secular arguments, to appeal successfully to evangelical Christian voters. In the midst of the generational shifts in the evangelical community, Democrats should press their case vigorously and search diligently to find areas of agreement about common goals for the nation.

We need to concentrate our minds on what is coming, not what is fading. We must not allow the bitter memories of recent feuds to cripple our actions and thoughts concerning the new political dynamics of the present. Of course, there will be some evangelicals who will never join us. Their personal views would no doubt preclude that. And heavy majorities in our party take justifiable pride in the great advances we have achieved for the nation on gay rights, for instance. But Democrats need to have faith in ourselves, as a first step, and that means returning to our essential nature. If we are to be true to our myth of being the Party of The People, then Democrats of every instinct have an obligation to draw in all people who have something to contribute to our cause, and this includes people of God. These are value-driven people; their politics is purpose-driven. They feel the need to act in the public arena because of how they read the Bible in light of the Social Gospel. They have the political instinct for explaining themselves by expressing the ethical frameworks that underlie their policy positions. There are many areas, beyond the hot-button issues that have split us in the past and probably will continue to split us, where Democrats and white evangelicals can find agreement and forge alliances to further causes on which we agree. The Party is open. They should come in and make their case.

And when they do, people on the secular side have a responsibility to examine what is being said and the context in which it is being said, instead of reacting reflexively and disrespectfully.

Not every mention of God in a public forum is a desecration of Jefferson's legacy. Not every reference to a passage in the Bible is a trumpet call from Joshua at Jericho, designed to bring the wall between state and religion crashing down. Some are. Some aren't. Just because these dangers might lie in wait is not a reason to foreclose the discussion at the start. As the believer must not shut down the words of the nonbeliever, so the nonbeliever must not shut down the words of the believer. The point is that people should speak their minds clearly and explain their underlying philosophical motivations honestly. They should be able to enjoy a well-grounded confidence that the Democratic Party wants its adherents to speak up freely. All Democrats should be open to learning from their fellow partisans.

We must decide what kind of party we are to have: a party whose overriding concern is that we all feel comfortable with one another because our views are predictable and familiar and we share the same instincts for getting into politics in the first place? Or a broad and accepting party with the self-confidence to confront its disparate instincts and take the very best from them?

William Jennings Bryan offers modern Democrats the fundamentals of a reasoned, impassioned response to the public religiosity of our opponents. The political myth of the Social Gospel may not be for everyone within the Party. Its ideas will disturb some and leave others cold. But parts of its moving impulses can be spectacularly helpful in clarifying people's minds about public issues and moving them forward together as Democrats.

The trouble is that we have abandoned this field. We have abandoned too many of our fellow Americans who draw deep sustenance from this ideal. We have abandoned Bryan. Yet William Jennings Bryan is worthy of our meditation. He found a despoiled republic. He mobilized millions in worthy fights to destroy a corrupt public culture and prepare its rebirth in justice. He appealed to the People's faith and idealism. He used the English language magnificently in the service of good, and many of his words were the old words. He imagined an active future for our philosophy of government. The Democrats' political Moses, he pointed the way to our great reforms of the twentieth century. He saved our party once. He can help lead us home again.

4

A RESPECT FOR IDEAS

Woodrow Wilson and Democratic Progressivism

The Democratic progressives of a century ago founded their politics on the determination to clear obstacles away so that The People could express their will and make it count. To that great battle against both public corruption and the power of overreaching private wealth, the progressives brought a profound respect for ideas, and particularly a belief in the ability of the technically well-educated to show the way forward to responsible reform. Here rests the core political faith of the modern-day Democratic progressive: discovering the public good by taking the advice of the expert.

He has pocketed the 1912 Democratic nomination for president. The Grand Old Party has split down the middle between the traditional Republicans who maintain their loyalty to business and the new progressives. Statistically, therefore, the Democrats have a practical shot at capturing the White House for the first time in twenty years. He has sorted out the big internal squabbles of his staff; the sums to finance his drive will be handsome, and they will be clean as well.

Technically, therefore, he is in good shape.

AUGUST 28, 1912: WILSON AND BRANDEIS
IN THE LONG AFTERNOON

But now, at the end of August, the governor of New Jersey suddenly realizes that he is a man in peril of his political life. Woodrow Wilson is about to blow his chance. His campaign is cratering. He is failing to touch the spirit of the American people. His arguments find but tepid response among the public. He sounds weak and confused. His rivals may be split, but so are his followers, and drastically so. The crux of the problem is that Wilson seems not to be able to figure out how to satisfy both the archconservatives and the archprogressives of his own fractured coalition. And perhaps even more critically, he doesn't yet have the public master key to distinguish his positions from those of his chief progressive rival, Theodore Roosevelt. Wilson has the "me-too" problem. It looks like the charismatic TR may be coming back to the White House.

The failure of Wilson's summertime 1912 presidential campaign is a failure of ideas. Now, just before Labor Day, Wilson will rescue his campaign, root his party, and revive his country. He will solve all his big political problems at once—and he will do it with ideas.

On August 28, 1912, Wilson quit the public fight and went into seclusion behind closed doors. There he took counsel with one of the greatest champions of the Common Man in American

A RESPECT FOR IDEAS

history. This was the Boston lawyer Louis Brandeis, whom Wilson would ultimately place on the Supreme Court. Alone during lunch and through long afternoon hours, the two men turned over in their minds the strategic problem of the fall race: how to sweep in the energized, ideas-alive progressives; how to hold the old South; how to check the dervishlike TR; what the key to the West was (always, Wilson was interested particularly in the West); and especially the question of how raw economic power in America really worked, and how it might be made to stand as the symbol of the problem of American democracy itself. No exact record exists of what they said to each other, and Wilson's biographers even disagree about where the meeting took place, whether in Trenton or in the governor's summer residence at Sea Girt on the Jersey shore. Yet the talk the two of them had would turn out to be one of the most fateful in American political history.

After his searching talk with Brandeis in the back room, Wilson re-emerged onto the public stage in Buffalo, New York, for his Labor Day speech, and there he began to conduct—indeed, even to command—the greatest presidential campaign in American history, bar none: the most emotional and thrilling, the most articulate, the most honestly stated clash of fundamental ideas about the meaning and form of American society and governance ever to be put before the citizenry of our country.

Wilson engineered a fugue-like politics that masterfully embraced the furthest contradictions of his party. As his campaign gathered steam, even the most radical progressives could see their fondest dreams of thoroughgoing economic reform at work in the substance of Wilson's program. The most devout Jeffersonian stalwarts could hear Wilson compare the Democrats to TR's progressives when he said, "Ours is a program of liberty; theirs is a program of regulation." His speeches took the driest

principles of macroeconomics and wove from them a heart-
pounding narrative of American democracy, where people come
before property, where the individual stands firm before the
giant machinery of the money combine and those who stand at
its levers of control, and where The People in their sovereignty
decide the rules of the contest in open legislative debate and
voting, instead of entrenched elites in their secret, off-stage
negotiations. Academics still argue over Wilson's campaign even
now, a hundred years on: Was he attacking from the left, or
from the right, or from straight down the center? In 1912, Wilson
waged the campaign that still stands today as the supreme
example of the decisive influence that ideas and ideals exert over
the outcome of power struggles.

In November, Wilson crushed Roosevelt and President Taft,
and he brought in heavy Democratic majorities on Capitol
Hill. The New Freedom was born.

Yet with the Democrats, always irony: out of the era of the
founding progressives, hallmarked by their rational approach to
reform, was to come a transformation of the progressives' own
fundamental myth, which had enshrined a respect for ideas, and
would make of that myth the forefather of today's modern confusion in politics, sapped of its clarity and emotion.

1912: THE PROGRESSIVES SPLIT APART

The election year of 1912 is most famous for the once-only split
it caused in the Republican Party, between William Howard
Taft and Teddy Roosevelt. But more interesting, and for modern Democrats much more momentous, is the rupture that cracked
the progressive movement wide open that summer, with some

progressives moving to the Bull Moosers and Roosevelt, and some moving to the Democrats and Wilson. The implications of this progressive breach still define, and still bedevil, the politics of the Democratic Party today. It makes a difference now whether you are a progressive in the tradition of Woodrow Wilson or a progressive in the tradition of Theodore Roosevelt.

The decisive issue of the 1912 campaign was the growing power of the giant corporate trusts that were beginning to dominate the American economy. Wilson and Roosevelt each agreed in principle that something had to be done to check this concentration of wealth. Each man was a progressive. Each man counted millions of progressives among the ranks of his followers, but it was clear to all that those progressives who had not yet made up their minds how to vote were likely to decide the election. The critical political problem of the campaign, therefore, was how to capture the swing vote of the undecided progressives.

Wilson and Roosevelt wound up disagreeing on how to attack the problem of the trusts. Their disagreements over this issue reflected their own personal political temperaments, which were very different. Their disagreements also reflected the very different political dynamics of the partisans who were backing their election. The philosophical differences that underpinned the progressive division between Wilson and Roosevelt a century ago reveal a great deal about the internal political dynamics of the Democratic Party today.

It's easier to understand Roosevelt, his temperament, and his political problem, than it is to come to grips with Wilson. Roosevelt had made his name as a progressive in general, and as a trustbuster in particular. He broke with Taft and the establishment Republicans because he felt that they had not continued the progressive policies he had laid down during his own time in the White House. The people who followed TR out of the Republican Party were pretty much all progressives. In 1912, therefore, he had a political party all of his own, with no troublesome dissenting factions to bedevil his personal instincts and decisions, all aflame with the surefire confidence that allowed him to proclaim, perhaps portentously, "We stand at Armageddon, and we battle for the Lord."

His temperament was forceful and direct; his approach to problems was straightforward. He took challenges head-on. He saw a problem; he took private, well-informed advice; and he acted, often alone. He was used to getting his own way. During his tenure as president, between 1901 and 1909, he was able to impose his programs on a grudging and often horrified Republican Party largely through the force of his personality. He was a political moralist. His politics reflected his temperament.

Woodrow Wilson's politics also reflected his temperament, but Wilson was a more complicated man, and his supporters presented much more complicated problems than Roosevelt's did. Wilson had a sure understanding of practical political problems because, unlike Roosevelt in 1912, he had an incredibly diverse coalition of political, cultural, geographic, and economic interests to try to manage, and to say that these interests were antagonistic is an understatement of the first order. Internal Democratic politics today is a game of patty-cake compared with the challenges Woodrow Wilson faced from his own supporters. He was to prove himself perhaps the greatest balancer of interests in the entire history of the Democratic Party. See him at work on the political high wire: marshaling his constituencies from the old bourbon South and the new progressive West; calling in the teeming North, both the urban machines and the earnest suburbs; rallying the foreign-born as well as the native; bringing the best out of the academy; running his partisan appeals straight through from the Sunday-go-to-churchers to the smart set of new secularists. The Democrats were all over the place; the Bull Moosers were a pure play.

By contrast with the command-and-control Roosevelt, Wilson had the temperament of a master legislative tactician. What really interested him was how to bring distinct constituencies with differing ideas into alliance with each other, when at first glance their interests and ideals appeared to clash irreconcilably. He was a symphony conductor rather than a soloist. He certainly had the progressive's respect for ideas. He had spent his entire career in the academy; he was probably the greatest academically trained intellectual we have ever had as president. Like Roosevelt, he often displayed the instinct of the political moralist— the rigidity of his political moralism was what wound up destroying him in the League of Nations fight—but in his approach to the problem of the trusts in 1912, Wilson was to cast himself as political economist rather than adopt the punitive political moralism of his progressive opponent.

In the fall of 1912, Theodore Roosevelt stood for what he called the New Nationalism. The deeply conservative Roosevelt was offended by the growth of the giant business trusts and correctly perceived them to be a threat to the state. Directly in Alexander Hamilton's line of thought, Roosevelt now had his eye on how to bolster the central state. Principally, he wanted to construct a strong central state for the muscular exercise of American power abroad, but he also understood the advantages that could flow at home.

Roosevelt explicitly accepted that monopolistic corporations would continue to exist and practice their trade-restraining ways, but he realized that some of the trusts had gone too far, and these would have to be reined in. If some of the trusts needed to be checked, he reasoned with straight-line logic, we must place more power in the central government and then employ that power to regulate those trusts whose behavior was becoming antisocial. Case by case, one by one, the state and the corporations were to work it out. The problem Roosevelt saw was how to reach an accommodation between the power of government and the power of business, with government and business being the actors, while everyone else would have to abide by their agreements. TR's state was the state as protector of the public mass. It was the English Tory model: the nanny state. Thus, Roosevelt proposed strengthening the central state so that it could regulate individual trusts and prosecute them in the courts, as might be needed.

With a much broader and more diverse coalition to hold together than TR's, Wilson took a radically different view. It was a fool's errand to try to regulate the monopolistic power of individual trusts, as his opponent proposed. It would amount to a wild-goose chase among the various hive-like trusts, which by then numbered in the hundreds. (TR, the touted trustbuster, had employed but five lawyers in the Antitrust Division of his Justice Department to fight them all; William Howard Taft brought more than twice as many antitrust cases as Roosevelt did.) This approach could not be effective. The power of the trusts was too deep and the crisis of the trusts had become too complicated for TR's piecemeal solution to work. Indeed, Wilson even went beyond the problem of individual monopolies, and began to raise the dark specter of "the combination of combinations" in the American economy.

To aggrandize the central state, to empower the operators of the bureaucratic apparatus to prettify the behavior of discrete and unique trusts—this smacked of a father-knows-best paternalism and an unseemly willingness to hand the whole problem over to a tiny handful of America's elites, cozily ensconced in the government and in the corporations. In fact, Roosevelt's policies would have allowed most of the trusts to continue operating. No. Wilson would not have it. He would demand justice.

And so, Wilson proposed that competition itself be regulated. It was the whole system of economic conglomerates that Wilson proposed to attack, with a comprehensive antitrust framework—not a frantic, endless, scattershot pursuit of wrongdoing by individual companies that might be taking unfair advantage. This proposition reflected the decisive contribution that Brandeis's advice had made just before Labor Day: go after the system itself; fix and reform the whole underlying structure; don't be distracted by an effort to lock up hundreds of bad actors. In Wilson's conception, therefore, isolated monopolies and trusts would not be regulated. They would be smashed: all of them. This was the only sure way of restoring fair competition and leveling the playing field so that every American had the chance to get ahead in life. This was the New Freedom of the Democrats in 1912. It was our counter to TR's New Nationalism. The Democrats' program was far more radical than the one proposed by Roosevelt and his Bull Moose Party.

And when he took office, Woodrow Wilson put through the greatest series of economic reforms in American history since the Treasury tenure of Alexander Hamilton and before the New Deal of the second Roosevelt. Wilson's New Freedom legislation was a thorough and all-encompassing expression of the progressive impulse, embracing structural reforms of the entire economy, as well as detailed reformations of specific sectors. The Clayton Antitrust Act of 1914 struck at economic concentration by bolstering the Sherman Act and intensifying the attack on monopolistic practice while removing organized labor from the threat of antitrust prosecution. The federal income tax; the slashing of the tariff across the board; the reform of the currency and the establishment of the Federal Reserve System; the Federal Trade Commission; rural farm credit; workmen's compensation; a national legislative attack on child labor; and Wilson's settlement of a nationwide railroad strike, establishing the precedent in law for the eight-hour workday—these reforms were the fruit of the progressives and their allies within our political party. They became law under a government of Democrats.

THE PROGRESSIVE CONTRADICTION: POPULAR SOVEREIGNTY VS. EXPERT CONTROL

The progenitor of Democratic progressivism is Woodrow Wilson, not Theodore Roosevelt. The foundational ideas of the early Democratic progressives were embedded solidly in the primacy of the individual citizen in America—pure Jefferson. And this core principle Woodrow Wilson understood ardently, from his early religious education as a serious Presbyterian, with all its emphasis on the individual's responsibilities to God and the duty to act with moral rectitude in society, and also from the intense southernism of his youth. Wilsonian progressives were determined to fight the giant business trusts in order to protect the individual citizen from overreaching economic power. In their fight for the individual, they saw that control by The People was what was really at stake—the fate of American democracy itself. This is what gave the early progressives such amazing emotional force: they had touched a primal American fear—the fear of authority.

And for these middle-class reformers, so zealous in their conceptions of cleanliness in administration, there was also the fear that the very weapon of The People, government itself, had been corrupted and rendered null by the go-to political boss of the city and his crooked political machine (and, we might note in passing, this usually meant the Democrats' crooked political machines, our very own). Indeed, the progressives saw menace in the possibility that these two dangers were amalgamating, with powerful businesses, in effect, buying politicians as they might buy other raw materials to feed their supply chains. The progressives were determined to smash both threats to American democracy: the private threat of the corporate trust and the public threat of the political machine. The progressives wished to make America safe, once again, for rule by The People, with the individual citizen at the center.

But there was a second progressive temperament, which was at war with the first. Many progressives wanted something more than clean government by The People. They wanted each matter to come out the way they thought that it should. The reform itself could become more important than how it was arrived at. Here was an embarrassing dilemma: What if the People didn't agree with the reforms the progressives wanted? What then? It could be an awkward pass, this place where progressivism and popular control might clash. This was the contradiction in the mind of the progressives, and they needed a way out. They found one. They made a new political myth, and it was a myth that carried the risk of threatening the viability of the first Democratic myth of popular sovereignty: *the myth that the expert knew best.*

Just maybe, this kind of progressive began to think, just maybe there were some kinds of problems the People didn't want to be bothered with. Maybe there were some kinds of problems that were so complex that the People wouldn't have the wherewithal or the technical ability even to begin to think about them. And then, no one could really argue with the proposition that sometimes the People got carried away by their emotions, or applied their own private self-interest a little too narrowly, or somehow fell short of the judiciousness necessary to appreciate the complexities involved in arriving at the overall public interest. In these kinds of situations, maybe a different way to make society's decisions was in order, a new way that could push the desired reform through, while at the same time avoiding the grubby give-and-take of politics, which might foul the whole thing up. The progressives were on to a certain truth in all this, but it was a half-truth, and it carried, therefore, real dangers for a country like ours. In any event, the progressives' solution involved removing some kinds of decisions from the hands of the People, and placing them elsewhere: into the hands of the expert, who was educated and trained to ascertain the best interests of the public. Indeed, lots of decisions, and more all the time.

This is an implacably logical temperament that cherishes results before all else. It believes that there are right answers, and that it has the right answers at hand. This progressivism is a top-down affair to be managed by society's elites. It operates alone whenever it can, to the extent that it can. It is a follow-the-leader model. Thus, its essential temperament is managerial instead of political.

This side of progressivism enshrines the role and power of the expert. This brand of progressivism is from Theodore Roosevelt's side.

Thus, two opposing temperaments, with distinct intellectual roots, inside the progressive movement itself: the early Democratic progressives marched under the old Democratic banner of popular sovereignty and, at times, even direct democracy. This was the impetus behind progressive reforms such as the direct primary, the popular election of senators, and referendum, initiative, and recall. Yet at the same time, there were other progressives who didn't march under the banner of popular sovereignty—quite the contrary. Progressive reforms such as city-manager municipal government; commissions of appointed public-spirited citizens with real decision-making authority; the increasing use of so-called blue-ribbon grand juries—juries not of one's peers, but composed of members of the smart crowd, right-thinking jurors who brought their own well-informed views into the jury box and made the right decisions and made them fast—all these proceeded from an entirely different impulse, one still aimed at defeating the skullduggery of well-organized vested interests, but operating nevertheless through mechanisms at the opposite end of the spectrum from direct democracy.

After Wilson departed the scene in 1921, the intellectual contradiction at the heart of the progressive movement remained. More than a century after Woodrow Wilson and Theodore Roosevelt took the stage, the Democratic Party continues to struggle with these two temperaments of its inherited progressive myth: the claims of popular sovereignty and the claims of expertise, and when to serve the one and when to serve the other. And sometimes today internal Democratic politics seems to play out as if the contradictions that Wilson succeeded in encompassing are now unbridgeable: you buy into more of one side, you get less of the other side.

This was exactly the danger that the progenitor of Democratic progressivism foresaw in the very beginning, and which he warned the citizenry and the Democratic Party to guard against. Wilson insisted on maintaining a balance between the principle of The People's control and the invaluable contributions that well-educated progressive experts might make to the public debate and formation of government policy. But for Wilson, the individual and The People had to come first, not the expert.

Wilson and the Democrats thus attacked the whole problem of economic injustice and concentration of wealth from a decisively different perspective than the one TR proposed. In relentlessly attacking the special interests of his day, Woodrow Wilson declared his core progressive faith by expressing his Jeffersonian and Jacksonian roots. The Democrats insisted on the sovereignty of The People to establish openly what the rules of the whole economic game would be, instead of trusting to the good faith of elitists in their secret backroom negotiations. The root of the Wilson approach stemmed from the Democrats' Jacksonian need to fight for the outsider, but also, critically, their fealty to the political myth of popular sovereignty, their instincts as the Party of The People. For the Democrats, this was received political wisdom. This fundamental idea did not—and does not today—have the same hold over the Republicans.

Therefore, Wilson was going to go to The People and have them set the rules of the economic contest in society. He would get the Congress to reform the economic system itself, instead of endlessly chasing its operators through the maze of the courts.

In 1912, he railed against TR's high-handed progressivism as hostile to a government of and by The People. Roosevelt's program would lead inexorably to "a government of experts," as Wilson declared, with cutting disdain. He would use the Democratic Party—The Democracy—to block the imposition of a system where The People would become puppets of a "National Board of Guardians."

What really happened in 1912 was that Theodore Roosevelt, blinded by his own command-and-control temperament and beguiled by the comfort of dealing only with his like-minded progressive supporters, had allowed himself to be placed on the wrong side of popular sovereignty, and Woodrow Wilson, at the head of the mighty phalanx of the Party of The People, proceeded to exact a just and decimating retribution. That's how the Democrats beat TR that year. It is a lesson Democrats should keep in the forefront of their minds today. It is a bold and perilous act of politics to trifle with the ideal of The People's sovereignty in a country like ours. Especially for the political party whose essential nature inheres in this exact bedrock faith.

WHAT HAPPENED TO THE PROGRESSIVES—AND HOW THEY BOTH WON AND LOST

The moment of Wilson's political dominance was brief. When his health collapsed amidst the wreckage of his League of Nations dreams, it was as if the country pivoted with buoyant and relieved determination to erase Wilsonianism from its collective mind. Off with Wilson and all his high-minded calls to duty at home and responsibilities abroad, and on to Harding, Coolidge, and Hoover, as the Republicans mindlessly meandered the nation through the twenties toward its end-of-decade cataclysm. So much for Wilson, and, so it seemed, so much for the progressives.

The progressives were finished in the Republican Party—Teddy Roosevelt himself had unceremoniously booted them out, with good riddance, in 1916. That year the establishment wing of the GOP reasserted its natural dominance and nominated an archconservative for president. The progressive Republicans rebelled and appealed to Roosevelt as their leader. But this time TR sided with the ultraconservative regulars, and told the progressives to fall in line behind the new standard-bearer, or get out of the Party. They left, for good. Now they were finished as a national force, surviving only as a local presence in states such as Wisconsin and Nebraska and scattered here and there across the country in some municipalities.

Their remnant stayed on with us, but even as they often operated the great institutional bureaucracies of the New Deal, their theories were in eclipse under Franklin Roosevelt, who insisted, as Wilson had before him, that the progressives had to remain harnessed to bigger elements of the Democratic coalition. Truman, who idolized Wilson, nevertheless trusted to his own instincts, which were largely the instincts of a machine politician, and, with some noticeable exceptions, he remained unimpressed by the claims of the credentialed progressives. Lyndon Johnson conducted what might almost be called a vendetta against the fashionable instincts of the progressives inside his coalition, resenting and mistrusting them and keeping them at bay, even as he called on them to design and manage many of the Great Society's programs.

Based on a record like this, the ultimate fate of progressives would seem to have been sealed. If you had had the taste for betting on politics, you would have placed your chips against them. And yet, you would have lost your money. It didn't turn out that way. Not at all. Instead, the progeny of the first flowering of the progressive era enjoyed a renaissance in our party. The underlying story of the Democratic Party since the Second World War has been the resurgence of the progressives. Leaving aside Truman and Johnson, and Hubert Humphrey in 1968, all of whom understood the politics of the country primarily through FDR's New Deal paradigm, every single one of the Democrats' post–World War II presidential nominees has come out of the progressive movement within our party; that's fifteen out of eighteen, from Adlai Stevenson in 1952 straight on down through Hillary Clinton in 2016. They exercise their influence through the sheer force of their numbers and the alacrity of their civic engagement. They have been manning the levers of control in the Democratic Party for quite some time now. It has allowed them to shape the rhetoric of the modern Democratic Party with their own concepts and their own terms of reference.

As the influence of the progressive cohort within the Democratic Party has grown over the past half-century, the faith of the progressives in the value of expertise has also grown. The result is that modern-day progressives have wandered from their early Wilsonian moorings, which recognized that progressivism had to root itself securely amidst other ideals of the Democratic credo. In effect, they have shifted from the Wilson side of progressivism to the Teddy Roosevelt side. And so it is that when contemporary Democratic figures like Bill Clinton and Barack Obama wish to signal their progressive instincts and loyalties to that part of today's Democratic coalition, it is the name of Theodore Roosevelt that they call. This betrays their current progressive temperament for the top-down, managerial fix, the accommodation among elites, the loner's decisive stroke: in other words, the world view espoused by TR, that the expert knows best.

Today's Democratic progressives believe in the intrinsic value of policy expertise for governing, but they have added something else on top of it. They believe that the way to attract the mass support they need in open political battles is to couch their appeals in the detailed language of public-policy positions. That is how they insist on conducting their fights in the public arena. Their idea is that they can thereby demonstrate that they are being serious and substantive and practical, showing their respect for both ideas and for the electorate they are trying to convince. They would have others believe that the very precision and specificity of their policy positions lend credibility to their promises, laying forth a standard by which the voters can judge them that is far sturdier than the vague old bromides, grudges, and pious hopes politicians have so often employed in the past.

For the progressives, therefore, politics has become more or less equivalent to policy and policy positions. This is how they were educated in school; this is the paradigm for politics they carry in the privacy of their own minds; and on this idea they stake their claim to the public's allegiance. The country has a problem, they say; here is the precise way we would propose to solve it, and if you agree with the specific solution we are articulating during this campaign, vote for us. Fair enough: it all seems straightforward.

The trouble with this—and the 2016 presidential campaign was glaring proof—is that this approach isn't working anymore. Why not?

Policy is not politics. To be sure, the two are definitely and inextricably intertwined, and dependent upon each other, but, most definitely, they are not the same. Politics is the art of organizing and conducting the power struggle. Every American, no matter his or her position or station in life, has a valid and equal stake in the power struggle, and therefore the terms in which the power struggle is publicly conducted must be capable of being understood by all. The progressive Wilson instinctively understood this. The public conversation itself was critical, and a politician's disrespect for that conversation aroused his ingrained hostility. "My dream of politics all my life has been that it is the common business, that it is something that we owe it to each other to understand, and owe it to each other to discuss with absolute frankness," he said in September 1912, as he was beginning to hit his stride. "If we don't understand the job, then we are not a free people." Big, simple ideals such as all men are created equal—these are the emotional building blocks of a coherent and connected public debate that can proceed through time, over long decades. They are sturdy enough to provide an intelligible discipline to the national conversation, yet flexible enough to allow for changed circumstances.

By contrast, policy is ephemeral. It is all about details, and the endless details morph as political pressures shift, or factual circumstances change on the ground, or compromises get made, or election days come and go. What are presented as immutable policy positions and promises before the first week in November can be, and often are, overtaken by the second week.

The cold, technocratic language of temporary legislative posturing is incomprehensible to the citizenry in its detail, and its relevance to the real issues at hand can be obscure. It drains any sense of sustaining emotion out of the debate. Instead of moving citizens to action, it moves them to the sidelines. It shuts people out. The airless, stunted policy lingo so often heard from

modern Democratic politicians is too often deployed to obfus-
cate the real choices before The People rather than to clarify
them.

The electorate needs context, and a framework, and a dem-
onstration of honest instinct, and a welcoming invitation to join
together in a dignified conversation about the destiny of the
nation. When a voter doesn't understand the terms a politician is
using to frame his argument, that voter instinctively feels talked
down to and left out of the conversation, and what happens in
the ballot booth in November then becomes entirely predictable.

Woodrow Wilson had a brush with this exact strategic dilemma during his 1912 campaign. He began to sense that he was
going to win the election based on his approach to breaking up
the trusts, but at the end of September, he had a momentary loss
of self-confidence based on some scattered questions he was being
asked as he powered on toward the finish line. Just exactly, precisely, how are you going to bust up the monopolies? Explain your
proposed legislation. Desperately, he wired Louis Brandeis asking
for his views on the specific details of antitrust policy. After a
couple of days, Brandeis replied with a lengthy, substantive mem-
orandum. Wilson read it and immediately cast it aside, recognizing at once that it was a distraction and had no place in the
conversation about raw power that he was conducting with Roosevelt and the American voters. He knew enough to understand
that the how-to questions could come later, and that if he maintained fidelity to the broad principles he had stood for during the
campaign as he crafted his legislation, he would be all right, and
the country would understand the job he was doing.

The great political questions are about unequal power and
individual dignity and bedrock security. If you pose these
questions in terms of hyperspecific policy proposals for dis-

crete special-interest groups instead of making a public argument based on fundamental principle and philosophy for all Americans, you place a needless obstacle between the Democratic Party and its fellow citizens. This approach leads the Democrats—and the electorate—into a political hall of mirrors where context is impossible to grasp and perspective is impossible to achieve. This is not the respect for ideas Wilson and the early Democratic progressives displayed. It is a bewildering confusion, gratuitously engineered. The relentless progressive attempt to impose the intellectual prism and rhetoric of policy onto the problem of politics is an artificial exercise, and can feel that way to the knowing public it is designed to impress.

THE PROBLEM OF PROGRESSIVISM TODAY

Progressive Democrats dominate our party today. Yet too often the progressives dominate the Democratic Party by themselves, alone, and therefore the dominance they exert is an uneasy one.

The difference between the growing reliance of the modern progressive on expertise and all the other political myths of our party is that the progressive myth is essentially a technique rather than an ideal. Progressives believe in the expert and the value of expertise, but this is really a question of how to get things done, not a question of what exactly you should be trying to do, or where you are headed. Today, bereft of broad goals like economic justice or individual supremacy to direct their efforts in the political arena, the progressives too often make it hard to figure out where they seek to take the country.

The progressives pose a big problem for the voter: How can you rely on them to pick one set of experts over another? What are the fundamental principles the progressives apply to their problems, and how do they make the critical choices they arrive at in private as they set about trying to solve the public's problems? In the wake of the 2008 financial crisis that befell the country, there was a fundamental argument among the experts who were advising President Obama. Shall we deliver the technical fix to the banks? Shall we put them back just where they were before the 2008 financial crisis and get on with our lives? This was what some progressive experts, advising the president early on, insisted we had to do. Or must we reform the banks, apply radical surgery, cut out the cancer, and make sure it doesn't metastasize again? This was what other progressive experts, advising the president later on, insisted we had to do. Each group of advisors, the early ones and the ones who came along a lot later, could fairly and factually be defined by their affiliation with the progressive wing of the Democratic Party. The citizen had no practical way to influence the outcome of this important debate, or even to understand what was really going on between the experts who were arguing in economic code behind closed doors.

The modern-day myth of the progressive is inherently unsteady because it is no longer held together by sweeping intellectual principles that might guide its purposes. The progressives have replaced purpose with method, principle with expertise. Yet the impetus for the grand advance in politics must reside in service to big, mythical goals. As a result, the interventions of the progressives in our current political debates do not compare to the reforming zeal and mighty accomplishments that marked their entrance into American politics a century ago. There is a distinctly marginal quality to their proposals these days. Beginning in the 1970s and continuing on long thereafter, Democrats began to present themselves as technocrats of efficiency in government, seemingly more interested in how programs were delivered than in what the end objects of those programs were.

The result is a paradox: the progressives are the most powerful faction within the Democratic Party today, yet without a sturdy rudder to steer by, they are the most isolated, and isolation is the most grievous danger there is in politics. Isolation means a loss of understanding of other people's instincts, concerns, and needs. Intellectual isolation from differing strands of the broad body politic can lead the loner into single-minded pursuit of his own narrow enthusiasms. Needless to say, isolation can mean the loss of potential political allies. Axiomatically, it makes it harder to get your own programs passed, and help is harder to come by when you get into real trouble, as inevitably you do in politics.

It is when the progressives seem to operate by themselves that they pose a problem for the Democrats (and, parenthetically, a danger to themselves). The progressive today operates in a virtual thicket of expertise. Lost in the fine print, operating alone without a reliable internal political gyroscope or solid alliances within the Party, the progressive tradition itself is suddenly vulnerable to the interpretation that what it really amounts to is this: "Leave it to us. We know best. We're the experts. We will operate the apparatus by ourselves." This thought rarely occurs to the progressives themselves, but Democrats from other cohorts in the Party certainly have it quite clearly in mind: the beneficiaries of the progressive myth are the progressives themselves, since they are the better educated, by and large.

What the progressives and the Democrats now need to do is to return to the wellsprings of their own authentic intellectual ancestry—to the early progressivism of Woodrow Wilson and his political party, instead of the progressivism that flickered ever so briefly through the factions of our opponents. Democratic progressivism means respect for the primacy of popular rule by The People, understanding that they are but one part of a broad coalition of interest groups, and particularly of ideas and ideals, and that the key to their effectiveness must lie in making alliances with goal-oriented intellectual traditions within the Party's structure.

Of course, the other side of the progressive contradiction does have its merits. Policy expertise is critical for governing. Progressive Democrats respect ideas and facts. Progressive Democrats would not allow their party to deny the reality of climate change the way the Republicans do these days, out of sheer ideological inconvenience.

Expertise does have its place, but it must be kept in its place. It must be tempered with political wisdom. Political wisdom must guide the political struggle. This, Woodrow Wilson, the forefather of Democratic progressivism, understood. This, modern progressive Democrats could profit by learning to understand, again.

Among all the political myths of the Democratic Party, the modern progressive myth is unique. Its faith in experts and its reliance on their expertise are a method, a procedure, a way of governing, instead of a substantive goal of what the government should be trying to do or where it should be heading, as in "all men are created equal." This is its chief weakness as a political myth. But ironically, it is also its chief strength. Of all the organizing paradigms in the Democrats' intellectual tradition, the progressive faith, by virtue of the very fact that it is essentially operational by nature, is the one that marries the best and the easiest with our other ideals. Properly conceived and brought to reality, therefore, this is a major advantage for the progressives and for the political party that is their home.

THE SOLUTION: THE COMMON NARRATIVE
FOR THE PUBLIC ALLIANCE

The ultimate purpose of a party in a competitive democracy is to organize political thought in order to conduct the power struggle. Yet these days it sometimes seems as if Democrats are too exhausted even to try to forge a party that can hang together as an honorable, respectable, and serious national force of ideas. Instead, we seem only intent on the technical business of how to mobilize the various isolated factions of our party, one by one. We have lost, in other words, the view of how to practice big politics.

At virtually every level of government, the voters rejected the Democratic Party and the mind-set that it was offering to the public during the 2016 campaign. We are out now. This is our opportunity to think again, to reconsider who we are, and what our guideposts must be for our country. To squander this moment in petty distractions would be an unconscionable act of dereliction. Therefore, the Democrats must now construct a political argument, a public narrative, that can tie our very disparate ideals together. It is not enough to serve one myth, like Jackson's myth of economic justice for the outsider, or today's dominant progressive faith in expertise. The common story the Democrats tell our fellow countrymen must encompass all the pillars of the Democratic faith. This is the master key for our escape from the failing politics of today.

For some Democrats nowadays, Woodrow Wilson is but a

dim figure suspended in the century-old American amber of racial segregation and deplorable wartime plundering of civil liberties, but one need not endorse all of Wilson's specific, long-gone impulses in order to appreciate the merits of his approach to the political debate. And, in fact, it is his political approach that can be most useful to us today, as we try to figure out how to extricate ourselves from the broken Democratic politics of our own times. Earlier, we saw Wilson as a superlative balancer of the ethnic, geographic, cultural, and economic interests of the various elements within the Democratic coalition of his own day. Democrats today retain a rough-and-ready understanding of how to balance groups of people within their party. What made Woodrow Wilson different—and what makes him particularly valuable to Democrats at this moment—was his ability to perform a deeper kind of balancing: the balancing of ideals and political myths.

Major advantages flow to the citizen or active Democrat who approaches politics by thinking—and acting—in terms of fundamental ideals, principled goals, and ultimate purposes, and who focuses on how to put these pillars of faith together. These terms of reference are simple and emotional. They render Democrats understandable to each other and to the broader electorate. They are what enable Democrats to have a comprehensible conversation with the American people. If handled artfully, even contradictory ideals can be combined in creative ways to unify rather than drive apart a far-flung coalition party. Because ideals are so broad and flexible, they are the political glue that can be applied to make a party stick together.

Thinking in ideals also shows Democrats what is fundamental versus what is transitory. Persistence and determination in reaching the goal are to be prized and maintained; the details can often be traded. Thinking in political principles rather than the details of policies can be a helpful guide to negotiating with our opponents in other ways, too. It is a way to avoid insisting on details on the way into a fight, which can often lead to trench warfare and paralysis. A Democratic Party that embraces the wide eclecticism of its own mythological intellectual traditions will find that it has more broad principles to work with, as it seeks to advance its own purposes in negotiation with its opponents. Historically, the great purposes of the Democratic Party have been anything but narrow and hyperspecific. By listening for the echo of our own originating purposes, and, more importantly, by doing the hard work of updating our earlier fundamental creeds so as to make them serviceable to the present day, Democrats should find that we can make more headway in guiding the nation than we have been able to demonstrate lately.

When he campaigned for president in the fall of 1912, Woodrow Wilson accomplished a subtle and all-encompassing maneuver in economic myth as he framed the politics of the New Freedom. The fight, for Wilson, was not really between big government and big business, as it was for the Bull Moosers' Roosevelt, who expected the state and the trusts to work out harmonious relations for each other and the rest of society as a whole, submerging individual interest into a bureaucratically engineered commonweal. Instead, in Wilson's mind, the fight was for the individual.

The reason the interlocking system of trusts and banks had to be brought under public oversight was to allow the individual striver in America to have the chance to get ahead. Individual self-interest must be allowed to flower, and the duty of government was to provide the conditions for that flowering. Wilson's program was aimed at establishing a regime of free competition up front, so that the country and business could be spared the giant, clumsy, and intrusive apparatus that would be necessary to regulate each individual trust. It was freedom he wanted, not heavy, constant government control—no doubt, this last message was received as sound Jeffersonian wisdom and heard with relief among his southern and other conservative backers. Listen to Wilson on the problem of the single striver, trying to get a start in life and business, facing the system the banks and the trusts had erected:

> There has come over the land that un-American set of
> conditions which enables a small number of men who
> control the Government to get favors from the Government;
> by those favors to exclude their fellows from equal business
> opportunity; by those favors to extend a network of control
> that will presently dominate every industry in the country,
> and so make men forget the ancient time when America lay
> in every hamlet, when America was to be seen in every fair
> valley, when America displayed her great forces on the
> broad prairies, ran her fine fires of enterprise up over the
> mountain sides and down into the bowels of the earth, and
> eager men were everywhere captains of industry, not
> employees; not looking to a distant city to find out what
> they might do, but looking about among their neighbors,
> finding credit according to their character, not according to
> their connections, finding credit in proportion to what was
> known to be in them and behind them, not in proportion
> to the securities they held that were approved where they
> were not known.

You have to hand it to the guy. He could speak. He could write. He took his typewriter with him to the White House, and he was the last president to write his own speeches. Here, in this passage, stands Woodrow Wilson's iconic political invention, for whom he fought tirelessly in the public arena: the "man on the make." The energetic man on the make is Jefferson's individual and Jackson's outsider, through and through, fused together and updated by Wilson for his own day. For Wilson, he is the embodiment of the special character of America's democracy. His invention of the man on the make also enabled him to communicate directly with the guy out in the crowd, or the reader of the newspaper, so that he could show him he understood him personally, and his problems. No such political icon exists for the Democrats these days, and therefore the personal connection between the individual voter and our party is fading today.

Furthermore, Wilson refused to accept the given assumption of all American political history up to then, that Jackson (insider/outsider) must forever stand in opposition to Clay (self-made man/economic opportunity). Instead, he fused these two myths together. Wilson's man on the make, the energetic American individual (Jefferson), was fully capable of making his own way up the ladder under his own power (Clay), if only he, as an outsider, could overcome the insider's self-interested obstructions to his path (Jackson). But even as Wilson bowed in acknowledgment of America's older, individualistic, rural self-reliance, he had to demonstrate that he understood the new reality of America: a sprawling, adolescent, unstoppable world of complexity and mass organization in the economy. This meant more cooperation, and particularly a more active and assertive federal government, in order to deal with the economic problems of the new century, and specifically in order to smash the venal rules that consigned the outsider to the margins. (Again, Jackson.) This was what the new Democratic progressives wanted to hear.

Thus was Wilson able to serve the century-old purpose of the first, early Democratic Party, yet satisfy his surging progressive base. His program was radical and conservative at the same time. It worked. In his day, a century ago, Woodrow Wilson brought his party together by bringing the historical political myths of the nation together. Wilson brought his progressivism to bear against child labor and for the infusion of human rights into American foreign policy because he believed profoundly in the Social Gospel as championed by Bryan. He fought for the progressive Clayton Antitrust Act because he was a soldier in Jackson's fight for the outsider. He throttled the Democratic machine in his home state of New Jersey because he believed in preserving Jefferson's supremacy of the individual. He became a fusionist of myth.

The critical characteristic to take note of is how this early Democratic progressivism was deeply intertwined with other strands of the Party's intellectual traditions. Wilson invented ways to put all these constituencies together because he had to, and because he was interested in the question of how to do it, and because he believed in the public necessity of employing ideas and ideals to accomplish it. The progressivism of Wilson and the Democrats was thus a bottom-up affair. Here stands Woodrow Wilson, with the original Democratic temperament of progressivism, solidly embedded in a coalition of differing ideals, needing to work sympathetically with opposing ideas and constituencies in order to bring about the best policy for the commonwealth.

MARCH 4, 1913: WISDOM OUT OF
CONTRADICTION

On a cloudy March 4, 1913, the day he took the highest office, Wilson delivered perhaps the finest first presidential inaugural address ever given by an American president. In it, he demonstrated the power of embracing political contradiction. If you read the speech carefully, line by line, phrase by phrase, you find the tensions of the country exposed, not covered up or reassuringly swept aside. Jefferson's individual is there, but so is the community. The old and the new; the great and the petty; the claims of tradition and the claims of reform; the high ideals—but the poisons and the cruelties, also—"the groans and agony of it all . . . , the solemn, moving undertone of our life, coming up out of the mines and factories, and out of every home where the struggle had its intimate and familiar seat." Wilson was explaining the program he proposed to enact, and indeed he was explaining himself personally, and he was doing it in a way that showed you the quandaries and complexities behind his thinking. Thus, listeners could feel as if they were in on the silent struggles inside the mind of their leader, not just recipients of an onslaught of one-sided argumentation.

Listen to what was wrong with the America of a century ago. Listen to Wilson's words:

> The great Government we loved has too often been made use of for private and selfish purposes, and those who used it had forgotten the people. . . . There has been something crude and heartless and unfeeling in our haste to succeed and be great. Our thought has been "Let every man look out for himself, let every generation look out for itself,"

while we reared giant machinery which made it impossible
that any but those who stood at the levers of control should
have a chance to look out for themselves. . . . The Nation
has been deeply stirred, stirred by a solemn passion, stirred
by the knowledge of wrong, of ideals lost, of government
too often debauched and made an instrument of evil.

All this is the distilled essence of Andrew Jackson's myth (the
insider vs. the outsider, and the collusion of the entrenched, in
and out of government). Wilson meant to deal with these problems. He knew that his private agenda was radically reformist,
and he was to produce the public results that confirmed it.

Yet instead of frightening his audience with apocalyptic vi-
sions of change, the speech had a reassuring quality that wound
up comforting them instead. Listen to the way he explained
himself:

> Our duty is to cleanse, to reconsider, to restore, to correct
> the evil without impairing the good, to purify and humanize
> every process of our common life without weakening or
> sentimentalizing it. . . . We have made up our minds to
> square every process of our national life again with the
> standards we so proudly set up at the beginning and have
> always carried at our hearts. Our work is a work of
> restoration.

Again: "We shall restore, not destroy."

Wilson thereby demonstrated that he had reached an understanding that is critical for a politician of reform in a country
like ours, an understanding never arrived at by many of them.

Often, the best way to build political support for a reform is to present it as a restoration of what came before, rather than a radical departure into the void of an uncertain and unknown future. This is wisdom, not cynicism. Wilson was to deploy this understanding time and again in his very intentional politics.

It's more difficult to be a Democrat. We are operating inside a vast and diverse coalition of ideas and ideals, and usually our opponents are not. Therefore, our task as Democrats is to imagine and encompass the nation as a whole, not just one or two narrow and cohesive slices of it. For this reason, we have to be purposeful in seeking out and embracing our own internal contradictions.

The way to accomplish this task, Woodrow Wilson understood, was to deal in the currency of political myth, not in the footnotes. In 1912, he showed that you have to step back and offer a sense of perspective on the political struggle, and that if you step back just far enough, you can begin to see how there might be a meshing of interests instead of irreconcilable differences of ideology. The progressives of today, too often adrift in the details, have produced a bewildering and unnecessary confusion in our politics. The public has long since tired of the techno-jargon the progressive movement thinks in and speaks with. If left uncorrected, progressive persistence with by-itself policy politics will bring the progressive movement to the edge of collapse, ending its century-long record of great reforms in the nation's life. The forefather of Democratic progressivism offers us a way out of our contemporary perplexity: speak to the ideals of the People; impose the context of high principle on the debate; demonstrate common purpose across the boundaries of separate constituencies.

Seek the public alliance across all elements and ideals of the Democratic coalition by constructing the common narrative for the Common Man.

The Democrats: grapplers with balance by temperament; strategists in myth; masters of contradiction.

5

ECONOMIC SECURITY
FOR ONE AND ALL

Franklin Roosevelt and the Safety Net

*The core ideal that Franklin Roosevelt brought into the
Democratic Party and bequeathed to the nation held that
government would stand as the ultimate guarantor of each
citizen's basic economic security. Economic security for each
individual. And economic security for the whole community.
The overriding test FDR applied to his programs was whether,
as a practical matter, they worked or not. In serving the
sometimes contradictory goals of the New Deal and the
people they helped, the Democrats proved themselves to be
pragmatic experimentalists, first and foremost.*

Even now, Franklin Delano Roosevelt is the colossus of the
modern Democratic age. Of all the great heroes of the Democratic Party, FDR is the closest one to us today: closest in time,
and closest as a basic political reference point. His influence over
us is the greatest of any of the champions of our political tradition. His economic reforms were more thorough than were the

reforms of any of the others. The field of his endeavors was broader by far than any of his predecessors' has been in our history. The Democratic Party is part and parcel of his accomplishment, inextricably and ever bound to his works and to his person. The legacy of the New Deal, its service to the economic security of the American, is now a commitment of the federal government, but it is a commitment initiated by the Democratic Party, and it has been maintained and expanded by us over the past seventy-five years. The rearguard Republicans have fought us nearly every step of the way. Democrats are proud of the accomplishments of the New Deal, its legacy to the nation, and in all justice, we have every right to be, because that heritage is our very own. Yet things are complicated.

THE SOLDIER AT THE FENCE

On the night Franklin Delano Roosevelt died in the spring of 1945, his great labor secretary Frances Perkins went out among the citizens who had gathered at the White House fence to mourn his death. A young soldier was there. Later, she wrote: "The young soldier sighed as I nodded to him and, still looking at the house, he said: 'I felt as if I knew him.' (A pause.) 'I felt as if he knew me—and I felt as if he liked me.'" Franklin Roosevelt was a complicated man, but his mightiest works flowed from his simplest instincts and brought forth the warmest response from his fellow countrymen and -women.

Every single American instinctively understood the New Deal and what its essential purposes were. Yet there was no pre-cooked, centralized plan that came down from headquarters in Washington, D.C. If you read the record of the president's cabinet meetings, it's pretty clear that the leaders of the government were flying by the seat of their pants. There was no intellectualized philosophical stance. There was no climactic political battle that stood above all the rest, marked their minds, and set out their path for the battles ahead.

Instead, there was instinct—soul, if you will. And the first instinct was that *the People mattered*. There was the thought that the American people deserved to live in a good democratic society, and when FDR talked about what he meant by that, the best he could do was to say that the kind of society he wanted to see, that he was fighting to build in the midst of the most appalling wreckage, was one that was free, fair, and decent. Such instincts and words can seem awkwardly innocent today, but for the New Dealers of three-quarters of a century back, they were the true and workable guideposts for the Democratic Party. Instincts like these were just about the limit of what Franklin Delano Roosevelt believed in, but he believed in them so ardently and sincerely, and followed them with such determination, that he was able to establish a personal bond between himself and the Common Man—and his political party—unequaled in our history since Lincoln.

The quiet, straight-from-the-heart reflection of the young soldier at the time of President Roosevelt's death reveals a deep political truth, for his own day, and for ours. It explains how FDR could have been the architect of the vastest centralized governmental bureaucracy in American history, and yet, at the same time, the modern era's greatest devotee of Thomas Jefferson's political ethos. The New Deal was the biggest, most detailed, and most complicated bundle of governmental programs and policies in our entire national experience. Everyone recognized that Roosevelt's program was a mighty exercise in social solidarity—economic security for all. Everyone had to pull together in a common effort to beat the emergency. Thus, the essence of the New Deal was its inclusiveness. It didn't go primarily to the South because the South was the poorest. It didn't go primarily to the West because the West was the driest. The New Deal went everywhere, to all regions, and to all people.

Even so, Franklin Roosevelt's humane spirit and remarkably supple political mind were able to maintain a proper balance between the community and the individual. The genius of the New Deal was how it managed to convey two seemingly contradictory ideas to the American public, both at once. By updating the way America thought about who the individual was and what his relationship to the community and the government should be, Depression-era Democrats took their old Jeffersonian philosophy and made it relevant to their own age. They masterminded huge programs that threw millions into social solidarity with each other to face the crisis. Nonetheless, each individual among those millions could feel that the government's commitments and actions were focused directly on him personally, and his family, reaching right into his living room to help him when he was in trouble.

For the jeweler at his bench in Providence, Rhode Island, and the mother isolated in the hollow in East Tennessee, and the migrant laborers working their way up the Central Valley of California—such different people, living in such different worlds, each relating to the New Deal in a different way— Roosevelt did something amazing. He served them as individuals, but he connected them to each other, and to their government, and to a bigger idea. And so they followed him, and their children wound up following the Democrats, too, because they remembered, and they were all discussing politics with the same general frame of reference that FDR laid out for them in the time of want, when America began to act.

The New Dealers were measuring the value of their actions by their worth to the individual, just as Jefferson had laid that standard forth at the start. This is what the young soldier was saying, and millions agreed.

THE DEMOCRATS' MASTERSTROKE IN MYTH

President Roosevelt never had any Republican opponents of any consequence at all. His real enemy was the Depression. The economic downturn of the 1930s was not only much worse than the recessions all of us have experienced during our lives. It was different. When Roosevelt was inaugurated, the national income was half what it had been three years earlier, when the bust began. The things that form the permanent, stable landscape of a person's life, the psychological earth underfoot, had been suddenly stripped away. There were some 13 million people without jobs under President Herbert Hoover; about one-quarter of the workforce was unemployed when he left the White House. For millions, it was impossible to find work and support a family. Five thousand banks closed under Hoover, erasing 9 million savings accounts. The accumulations of millions of working lifetimes were wiped out in a second, through no fault of the depositor at the padlocked door. No economist's chart could explain the reality of the Great Depression. No economic plague remotely like it had ever been visited upon the nation before. In fact, Roosevelt took power in a radically dysfunctional era, with a crippled economy that had badly eroded the legendary self-confidence of the people of this country. He found a real emergency: economic, political, psychological. It was an emergency more calamitous than any other we had ever faced, excepting always the Civil War.

The critical element that FDR introduced to our party as well as to the country at that time was the commitment to economic security. The federal government would henceforth not permit a situation to arise where an American might fall off the last rung of the ladder and into the abyss. During a campaign radio address from Albany, New York, on October 13, 1932, about four weeks before the election, Roosevelt stated his bedrock political faith: "Modern society, acting through its government, owes the definite obligation to prevent the starvation or the dire want of any of its fellow men and women who try to maintain themselves but cannot." This was new. Only forty years before, Grover Cleveland had vetoed an appropriation of ten thousand dollars to buy seed for drought-devastated Texas farmers with the blindered assertion that "I do not believe that the power and duty of the General Government ought to be extended to the relief of individual suffering." Bryan had turned the Democratic Party in the direction of FDR's logical conclusion, but neither he nor Wilson could have envisioned such a sweeping commitment as the one that FDR advanced.

On March 4, 1933, Franklin Roosevelt took command of the United States government, announcing that "the only thing we have to fear is fear itself." During the next six years, he was to make the most active use ever of The People's government in behalf of The People, in ways that had been entirely unimaginable before he came to power. On that first day, he took command not only of the national government, but also, critically, of the national political conversation, and fired the imagination of America's citizens. Roosevelt set a sweeping goal during those dire years that energized the Democratic Party and the nation at large. FDR got the country out of the Depression, and he did it by producing a strong growth economy. He wanted more than stability and prosperity; he aimed for dramatic expansion. Economic growth would help him deal with equity and social-justice questions. In fact, this was probably the single most important idea Americans kept in their minds when they thought about the Democratic Party during the New Deal and for the next half-century: the Democrats were the party of domestic economic boom. Thus was FDR able to mobilize the working political majorities that put his great reforms through. President Roosevelt's primal idealistic principle was so compelling and resilient that it continued to organize and even dominate the struggle for power in this country until 1981. As an organizing framework, this political myth stood alone, unchallenged by any serious competing paradigm, for at least half a century. And FDR's political ethos endures today at full strength in the minds of millions of our fellow partisans and countless others besides.

It was the Democrats' masterstroke in myth for the modern age. We all love FDR.

FIGHTING OVER THE NEW DEAL

But the truth is that while all Democrats love FDR, no one agrees about what he means for the politics of today. Our record of dealing with his legacies has been decidedly mixed, marked by both justified pride and justified hesitation. So Democrats not only debate the Grand Old Party when it comes to the legacy of FDR; we also debate the merits of the New Deal among ourselves. We have never been able to reach a comfortable consensus within the Democratic Party.

When most people think about the New Deal now, including most Democrats, they see in their minds the agencies, the tomes of regulations, the public works, the big navy and army, the social security card and the money it brings, and the jobs, jobs, jobs. We can see the good these things have brought about in our country; we can touch them; we can feel their effect. They are tangible to us. We are proud. These things are ours. We fought for them over the persistent and bitter objections of the Republicans. We are the ones who helped make these things possible.

Yet these are the very things that we have fought over among ourselves for more than seventy-five years now. The Democrats of the North Alabama hills may have loved the rural hospitals that the New Deal brought, but they worried about government intrusiveness into people's personal lives. The progressive theorists of the Bill Clinton era produced macroeconomic charts demonstrating the need to do away with the welfare state, but the efficiencies were not so apparent in the projects of Southside Chicago, where the machine built its election-day victories. The traditional New Deal alliance of Democrats in the West, founded in extractive industries and the virtues of irrigation and massive public-works jobs programs—that coalition evaporated in the face of militant environmental dissent. All these fights—which have taken place inside the Democratic Party—have concerned the specifics of New Deal legislation and programs. In the beginning, the Democratic New Deal coalition was impregnable. Ronald Reagan ended that, but by the time he came along in 1980, the coalition was already unraveling, and the fights that finally busted up its political invincibility came over the details of FDR's programs from the 1930s.

Only three of our presidential nominees since FDR looked primarily to the New Deal as their political lodestar—Truman in 1948, Johnson in 1964, and Humphrey in 1968—but this is to understate drastically the influence of the economic-security imperative over the modern Democratic Party. During the last three-quarters of a century, our internal politics have largely been about trying to reach a workable relationship for ourselves with the accomplishments of FDR and their meaning and applicability (or lack thereof) to changing conditions. All Democrats have wrestled with this problem, and they wrestle with it still, even as the specific historical conditions that spawned the programs fade further from memory.

Harry Truman, fighting with his back to the wall in 1948, threw every political myth of his party into the autumn struggle with the Republicans that year, though naturally, for him, the New Deal myth dominated. Lyndon Johnson was almost the personification of the New Deal myth. The New Deal's promise of economic security was what he believed in, and he tried to serve it in just the same way FDR had served it during the Depression. This was how he governed. No one ever gets everything he wants in politics, but Johnson came pretty close. Everything that remained undone about the New Deal, everything that FDR and Truman had tried for but failed at, everything that JFK in his overweening caution did not even attempt—this was to be LBJ's great work in the White House. He gets the silent treatment from Democrats now, and ironically, his domestic legacy may carry an awkwardness today that might run even deeper for us than his foreign-policy legacy. In the space of four years,

Johnson's War on Poverty cut the national poverty rate by about a third. The party of FDR and LBJ could have done significantly better on getting rid of American poverty since then, over the past half-century, than we have.

Our other presidents of the post-1945 era stood more ambiguously to the side when it came to dealing with the legacy of FDR. John F. Kennedy had a curious but unsentimental mind, and you could see him begin to toy with the New Deal structure, but he didn't have time to work things through. Jimmy Carter was more judicious than most amidst the arguments swirling around the principle of economic security, more analytical than emotional, and therefore oddly, but to his advantage, a little distanced from the Party's central internal debate. He knew the whole thing had to be rethought, but he had neither the intellectual framework nor the ruthlessness to impose a new paradigm for the role of government. Half his people agreed with him about the need to scale back and pursue major efficiencies, but half didn't, and so he wound up tinkering around the edges rather than facing the whole thing head-on.

FDR'S TEMPERAMENT IS WHAT WE NEED
TO FOCUS ON

The Democrats have had a lot of problems with FDR's New Deal, and with each other, since the end of the Second World War, but there is a way forward through this conundrum for us, and that is to step back and recognize a larger truth: there was more than one New Deal. There was the tangible New Deal and there was the temperament of the New Deal. There was a visible New Deal and an invisible New Deal. For most of this time, we have been fighting about the visible, tangible New Deal. It is the embalmed New Deal that we have too often been trying to protect. I think FDR would have been puzzled by this. No doubt, he would have appreciated the intended compliment, but he probably would have been amused, too. I think he would have warmly encouraged the Party to move away from the old specifics, and on toward new solutions. He wanted to remove obstacles, psychological and traditional, economic and structural, that blocked the path to practical solutions for the country as a whole. He was a big man. He himself removed his own solutions when they got in the way of overall progress.

This was to be the pattern of his New Deal: jumping here, jumping there. He maintained a theoretical belief in the concept of a balanced budget, for instance, and tried it once, in 1937, only to watch the economy nose-dive. He reversed within months and opened the money spigot in an attempt to reflate the nation's output. He curried favor with the business community in the early period, but when it stood aside and refused to cooperate with his program, he took it on. "They are unanimous in their hate for me—and I welcome their hatred," he said at Madison Square Garden on the eve of the 1936 election. "I should like to have it said of my first Administration that in it the forces of selfishness and of lust for power met their match. I should like to have it said of my second Administration that in it these forces met their master." For the political mind that demanded logic and consistency, the New Deal made no sense at all. The exasperated Republicans, of course, painted him as a charlatan, with his constant pirouetting this way and that, but the country never bought it. The common man and woman stuck with him, no matter how much chopping and changing he did.

They stuck with him because they believed down deep that

he was keeping his eye on the endgame: the government's great promise to guarantee every American's basic economic security. That was core for them, and they knew it was core for FDR, too. They didn't mind the details of his contradictory maneuvering, because what remained for them was a belief in the purpose behind the maneuvering. During the New Deal, the goal was never in question, but the path of approach to the goal was questioned every day, and that, in the judgment of the citizenry, was fine by them.

What allowed Franklin Roosevelt to operate this way? It was his temperament. FDR's program is often thought of as the most doctrinaire in our history, but it needs to be seen in a completely different light. Actually, FDR was the antithesis of doctrinaire, and there was nothing dogmatic or doctrinal about his program. It could not have been less European or ideological. It was, in fact, quite the opposite. It was opportunistic. It was pragmatic. It was flexible, determined to change with the shifting winds of political mood and economic performance. It had no truck with theory when theory was in conflict with results. It was optimistic amidst the most appalling difficulties. Its spirit focused on the hope and humanity of the country, not on the ugly realities in the wreckage of its dreams. We have never been able to agree about all the details of the programs in the New Deal, and we still can't today. Thus, the greater possibility for us now is to focus on the invisible New Deal, its temperament, and the temperament of its master.

To begin with, Roosevelt understood and liked people, and he wanted them to have what they thought they needed. Hence, a certain whiff of profligacy hangs about his legacy. "Why not?" he asked, when queried about employing artists on the public-works rolls. "They are human beings. They have to live.

I guess the only thing they can do is paint and surely there must be some public place where paintings are wanted." There was no First Amendment discussion here, no casual speculation among theories of whether art might corrupt government, or government corrupt art. It was the end good he wanted: he wanted food in their bellies and self-respect in their hearts and civic pride all about, and he wanted those things right away.

It is impossible to imagine someone like Bryan thinking this way. Bryan was dead serious about his end goal of helping the farmer to repay his debts, and he decided that inflating the currency was the way to get there. Wiping away the gold standard, therefore, became principle for him and it was paramount. It was as if the tactic had become the goal. It wound up destroying him. Roosevelt would have found this absurd. The underlying purpose was what interested FDR. He was interested in the currency only as a tool. If gold worked, fine; if it didn't, change it to something else. It was FDR who took us off the gold standard, right at the beginning of his administration. Shortly afterward, in his office with a group of senators from silver-mining states in the West who wanted more silver specie, he reared back with a big laugh: "I experimented with gold and that was a flop." (Note: a flop, not a Cross of Gold.) "Why shouldn't I experiment a little with silver?"

WE ARE THE EXPERIMENTERS

And here is the key word: experiment. When he was running for the White House in 1932, Roosevelt said practically nothing about what he would do if he won, but on May 22, when he got to Oglethorpe University in Atlanta, he included a tiny paragraph in a commencement speech that gave the show away. In retrospect it would become clear that he was telegraphing his instinct for how he would govern the country if elected. Here is what FDR said: "The country needs and, unless I mistake its temper, the country demands bold, persistent experimentation. It is common sense to take a method and try it. If it fails, admit it frankly and try another. But above all, try something."

The economic emergency made Roosevelt's approach to politics and governing different from those of his great Democratic predecessors. Each of the others was backward-looking in some sense: Jefferson looking back into the limited fields of a rural arcadia on the Virginia frontier; Jackson looking back to a sturdier age before governmental favor perverted the free man's chance to make his way; Bryan insisting that he was only harking back to Jefferson's and Jackson's verities, even as he was overturning the Party's most fundamental political philosophy of governing; Wilson looking back to an age before his man on the make stood under threat from the crushing power of the trusts and complexities of modern capitalism.

But Roosevelt—in some ways, certainly not in all ways—is not part of this line. He doesn't fit in with his predecessors the way Jackson, say, could fit in with Jefferson. Roosevelt's situation was genuinely and frighteningly new. He didn't have time to look back; he had to look ahead, instead. He had to act and act immediately. Franklin Roosevelt's only interest was in what worked. "Do something," FDR said. "If it works, do more of it. If it doesn't, do something else." FDR's Democratic Party was not the party of doctrine—big government or little government, regulation or deregulation, gold or silver, public religiosity or secularism, tariffs high or low. No. Roosevelt's party was the party of pragmatism.

President Roosevelt's head of relief was Harry Hopkins. Hopkins hired more than 4 million people at the beginning of the winter of 1933, and let them all go again when spring arrived in 1934. He summed up his whole philosophy and his job and what he thought he had to do to help those who were in trouble: "Feed the hungry, and goddamn fast!" Just get on with the job: put money in their pockets, and food in their mouths, and give them work to do building roads across the Middle West. If you could do that, dignity and philosophy would take care of themselves. This was the spirit of the New Deal. For FDR, the facts came first. The pragmatism of the New Deal was what ultimately forged the loyalty of the American public to the Democratic Party. What we offered, what we brought about—as a practical matter, it worked. That's why they stuck with us.

It was not the liberals who displayed high-minded prickliness about their principles and programs—there was actually very little of that among the New Dealers. Instead, they focused on building new organizations and institutions, and they molded them to deal with the new and frightening facts on the ground, not their own moral preconceptions. The New Dealers dropped the insistent moralism that had so marked the thinking of the progressives at the beginning of the twentieth century, and marks progressive thinking once again today. The huffiness was all on the other side—the "principled" Republican, conservative side—whose solons took to the hustings to make galumphing speeches about "the road to Moscow," while Roosevelt governed to save the country.

In American politics, we Democrats are the pragmatists. We Democrats are not in the line of Hobbes and the leviathan state, nor of Hamilton. We are not the theorists, and we are not the ideologues. We are the experimenters. We must remain so in

our current day and into the future. The danger and temptation
we can face lies in confusing goals with programs. Sometimes,
unthinking support for established programs and policies
can turn into vested, status quo politics. Absolutely, we must
continue to serve the core principle of economic security for each
American. That is our own political myth, and we must make
sure that whatever we do, we are successful in bringing help to
those who need it. But the method of implementing our myth
must be pragmatic, factual experimentalism.

Among postwar Democrats, the modern figure who understood this best was Bill Clinton. He couldn't dodge the difficulties posed by FDR and the New Deal because he was operating
in the immediate wake of Ronald Reagan's frontal attack on the
reigning Democratic myth. Politically, Clinton was a figure of
absorption. Or to put it more concretely, Bill Clinton was an
Eisenhower figure as president, and the weight of historical judgment these days makes that a compliment. Eisenhower, as the
putative GOP nominee in 1952, was determined to put the old
arguments behind him and pull his newfound party out of its
habitual ruts. He succeeded admirably in forcing the Republicans to declare a truce in their war against the basic programs
of the New Deal. Ike was able to get the Republicans to accept
some of it, albeit grudgingly. They didn't like it, but they did it.
They were thus absorbing the centrist philosophy of the Democrats' New Deal.

Just as Eisenhower guided the Republicans of the 1950s
toward a cease-fire with the New Deal, so Clinton guided the
Democrats of the 1990s toward a more objective and dispassion-
ate appraisal of Reaganism, and indeed of their own mythological heritage from the 1930s. Was more regulation always
best? No. Could there be circumstances where smaller govern-

ment was best for the country? Of course. The most famous political quote of his career is probably "the era of big government
is over." There was no greater New Deal hallmark than welfare
assistance to the needy. Nevertheless, Clinton struck a deal with
the Republicans to end it, amidst agonizing negotiations over the
exact conditions. He took heavy criticism for what he did at the
time, and a legitimate policy debate continues through today.
But he moved forward because he was convinced that the
system in place was not working to achieve the stated goals for
which it was established. Welfare programs themselves weren't
important to the president. The purpose of welfare was what was
important. In his own mind, he decided to serve the purpose
and not the instrument.

Clinton was thus the one who finally succeeded in getting
the Democratic Party to focus on the temperament of the New
Deal instead of on its tangibilities. He cleared away a lot of the
old defended-through-the-decades details, his welfare reform
proposal being the prime example of this approach. He asked
again the questions that Roosevelt had asked all the time: Is it
working? If it isn't, how can we make it better? What are the
new experiments we need to try? We aren't completely out of
this frustrating bind yet, but we are moving, and it was Clinton
who set us on our way. He did it with the pragmatic, experimen-
tal spirit bequeathed to us by FDR.

6

REDEEMER NATION

From John Quincy Adams to Harry Truman—
The Marriage of High Ideals and Hard Interests

The Democratic Party invented the dominant framework
for the conduct of American foreign policy. It is a
two-pronged paradigm: the marriage of high ideals—America
as Redeemer Nation with a special mission for good in the
world—coupled with hard national interests—the tangible
advantage to our power, safety, or money. Both elements of
this political myth are necessary to sustain the public's
support for any serious commitment by our government
abroad, and each side of the myth tempers the other side.

I am working alone in my office at the State Department in Foggy
Bottom at six thirty in the morning on Christmas Eve 1979.
The chattering news ticker to my right begins to ring insistently
and I glance up vaguely and wander over to it. A single sentence:
a line and a half. Then, the machine falls silent. I hear myself
draw an involuntary, sharp breath. I rip the sliver of paper from
the machine, and I am out the door, bolting down the yellow

corridor, turning left into the corridor with the strange candy-striped wallpaper, and heading to the elevators that go up to the Seventh Floor where my boss works.

ON THE SEVENTH FLOOR AT THE STATE DEPARTMENT

Once upstairs, still moving quickly, I pass the security men with an easy wave and approach the last desk in front of the open door. "I need him," I say quietly, "*right now.*" She nods me in. It is a very small office, the size of a tiny kitchen. There is a desk at one end and seats in the room for three, maybe four. The window looks out onto the Lincoln Memorial. Alone at his desk sits Jimmy Carter's secretary of state, Cyrus Vance, out of West Virginia by way of Wall Street and the law—clear of thought, sound of judgment, and clean of hand. I remember now that he was wearing a gray three-piece suit and a green-and-blue-striped bow tie that morning. He is reading the overnight diplomatic cable traffic. He looks up, smiles kindly, and we say good morning. I lay the sliver of paper in front of him, which he now reads.

He is a very erect and measured and controlled man, but at this point, he slumps forward silently and lays his head on the desk—just momentarily, only for a few seconds. Then, looking steadily at me over his reading glasses, he says: "I have been warning them about this for days. Now," he adds grimly, "there will be trouble."

It was the Soviet invasion of Afghanistan. I had brought him the news that Russian mechanized divisions had burst through the border posts and airborne troops were landing outside the capital city of Kabul. We had been following their buildup for about a week and a half, but now the Soviets had gone through with it. This was the news that would dominate my life over the next month: What was the U.S. government going to do about it, privately and publicly? What should we say? And how should we say it?

At noon on weekdays, I stepped to a press conference podium in the Department of State to deliver the official diplomatic positions of the United States, answer questions about them, and defend them, live and on the record, in open give-and-take. My job—with such understandings as I possessed about the politics and deeper missions of our own country, and through talks with my colleagues about what we were doing abroad—was to find the words to say all this. This is what would bring me to Secretary Vance's office, usually a couple or three times a day: at seven in the morning, again at a quarter to twelve, and sometimes at the end of the day, too.

The tacit underlying theme of many of our conversations in those days was the delicate question of how to incorporate the legitimate instincts of the American people into the policies of their government abroad. I was a political appointee in the Foreign Service, and my work placed me at the precise spot where domestic politics and foreign policy meet in a very public way. When I checked in for work at the Department of State in January 1977, I was under no illusions as to how I had arrived at my new post: I did know something about international affairs and foreign policy, but I knew that the real reason why I was there was because I had come up through the battles of home-grown Democratic politics in Virginia. And so one of the things that puzzles me now is that it never occurred to me then to ask myself whether there was such a thing as a Democratic Party foreign policy for the United States. Yet our own particular story is intriguing, and it is very different from the story of our opponents.

Even so, many Democrats today would probably like to believe that ours is the party of domestic focus and concern, secretly suspecting that in some vague, undefined way we are "better" at domestic affairs than foreign affairs. It is important to remember that our party was formed in a foreign-policy dispute, not a domestic one: the clash in the Washington administration at the time of the French Revolution between Secretary of State Thomas Jefferson, leaning to Paris, and Alexander Hamilton and his High Federalists, leaning to London. Right from the first day, therefore, foreign relations have been a crucial focus for our party, not just an ancillary distraction. Foreign policy has reinforced the solid reputation of the Democratic Party with the American people, as it did in the wake of the Second World War victory. And foreign policy has wrecked the Democratic Party, as it did in Vietnam, when our internationalist self-confidence was temporarily shattered.

The inquiry here is about a way of thinking. Its subject is a frame of reference, and therefore, a political myth. It is about the approach of the American mind—specifically, the approach of the Democratic mind—to the world outside. Now, after these many long and sometimes disappointing years, I realize that this is what Cyrus Vance was teaching me. Without ever mentioning the words "Democratic Party," he was bringing across to me the traditional Democratic paradigm for how America looks at the world, and he was emphasizing that each new generation needs to undertake the search for the modern meanings and applications of that paradigm. These were often the kinds of questions I needed to turn over with the secretary of state in his hideaway office, watching him reach for the common sense behind it all as he gazed from his window across to the Lincoln Memorial, and searching and struggling with him through the complications for the practical way forward.

THE DEMOCRATIC PARTY'S FOREIGN-POLICY MYTH MADE AMERICA'S PLACE IN THE WORLD

As it turns out, there is a foreign policy that is distinctive to the Democratic Party. We come from a worthy tradition. We come, in fact, from the nation's critical tradition in international affairs. For it is we, the Democrats, who have made America's place in the world. At each decisive moment, we have been the ones to step forward with the ideas and the framework to explain, as well as to sustain, the ways in which America must deal with the outside.

The nub of the foreign-policy problem, for Democrats, is this: How do we harmonize service to our tangible national interests with service to our intangible national ideals? Out of our party's historical traditions, we have developed a very specific foreign-policy lens for looking at America's role in the world. It is the fusion of America as Redeemer Nation—a belief in ourselves as a people with a special, idealistic, and exceptional mission in the world—and hard-edged national interest—the tangible benefit to our power, safety, or money.

Each one of the transformative Democratic foreign-policy mythmakers, despite being faced with wide-flung and radically different international puzzles, solved this problem in the same way: he married American interests to American ideals. By constantly reinventing this marriage, in new language and new concepts based on new realities, the Democratic Party has succeeded in establishing the terms and conditions of our nation's involvement abroad and in securing the support of the American people for those efforts.

This Democratic foreign-policy myth is based on a couple of basic political assumptions. First, for Americans, ideals, when they are primal enough, are real interests, just like money or power or safety. Our ideals are universal, we believe, and therefore we have a duty to enunciate them—and sometimes to act upon them and exert our power to bring them to fruition. But second, the two prongs of this paradigm are constantly influencing each other, the one ever tempering the other. Our idealism should leaven the crass self-interest that we, like all other nations, must serve. At the same time, however, our tangible self-interest should restrain us as we try to decide where and how to apply our power in service to our idealism, which otherwise would demand commitment everywhere in the world, with maximum force, because our ideals are, almost by definition, relevant to all peoples in all places.

Thus, the Democratic myth: an appeal to innate American idealism, coupled with a clear, widely shared understanding of American tangible interests. The two must go together; one without the other, either way, generally leads to diplomatic, political, and military collapse. Walking this line between interests and ideals is difficult and potentially even dangerous. But through long and sometimes bitter experience, Democrats have been brought to the realization that this political exercise has become a necessity for the success of American foreign policy.

Although we have succeeded, over the last couple of centuries, in establishing our own Democratic myth as the dominant paradigm for the conduct of American foreign policy, we have not been alone in this field. As you might expect, the Federalists,

Whigs, and Republicans have all tried their hand at it too. They have even prevailed in imposing their own version of a foreign-affairs framework from time to time—but only for the shortest time. Key words like "money," "glory," "dread," and "realpolitik" mark their alternative offerings to the American public. These considerations are important in the formulation and explanation of foreign policy, but our opponents have tended to endorse now one, now another, to the exclusion of other factors, and their mind is thus more simplistically constricted than ours is.

The money model runs directly back to Hamilton and the Federalists, and Calvin Coolidge's slogan "the chief business of the American people is business" sums it up. The flag follows the buck. The idea that the weightiest and clearly overwhelming goal of American foreign policy should be to advance the interests of American enterprise has been a serious and persistent, if not particularly idealistic, strain since the beginning. Republicans serve the interests of big business assiduously, either by tangibly assisting its specific needs, or by arranging the freest hand possible for its activities, depending on the reigning enterprise theory of the day. Of course, Democrats also mix the business interest with their other concerns; the last two Democratic administrations have served this tenet quite noticeably with their endorsement and facilitation of economic globalization. As a long-lasting and sustainable model for the nation's involvement with the outside world, however, the organizing influence of the Hamiltonian idea of placing paramount emphasis on financial interests has been problematic, even momentary: without idealism, a policy like dollar diplomacy, under which William Howard Taft sought above all to open foreign markets for American banks that wanted to loan money abroad, has always seemed to enjoy but a brief half-life.

Glory? Here stands Theodore Roosevelt. But glory is not necessarily linked to tangible interest, and in any event, it has a nasty habit of turning on you. TR was all for glory during the charge up San Juan Hill in Cuba, but he found it less to his liking after he helped shove us into the Philippines as colonial masters in 1898, thereby provoking a decidedly resolute insurrection.

As for realpolitik—power politics, in other words, plain and simple—since we are the most powerful, why not power politics? This view, in fact, prevailed under Richard Nixon in the late 1960s and early 1970s. It seemed quite sophisticated at the time, very grown-up, beguilingly European. Furthermore, this type of policy, bled dry of idealistic considerations, is geometrically simpler to operate than the dominant model of the Democrats. There was a certain surface elegance to the live-and-let-live underpinnings that lay behind the Republican policy of détente toward the Soviet Union, but it was essentially inert, and it did not satisfy the yearnings of Americans for principle and purpose in their work abroad. Its moment was brief, swept away by Jimmy Carter, who reasserted the primacy of the dominant model.

Now, with the 2017 advent of a Republican administration, realpolitik has made a new and momentary reappearance at center stage, and this time with a vengeance. It is a make-it-up realpolitik that can seem to go out of its way to disdain and even mock the traditional idealism of the American people and their concern for human rights abroad.

We get into trouble when the operators of our foreign policy become isolated from the complicated instincts of their fellow citizens. A political party cannot operate the foreign policy of the government, but it does have a role to play. One of its critical functions in our democracy is to serve as a mediating institution

in ideas between the citizenry and their government. After serving my years in the Department of State, I emerged with real
doubts about the wisdom of the old advice that politics must stop
at the water's edge, and a real conviction that the citizenry's oversight of foreign affairs experts and the foreign-policy establishment was much needed. The active and ongoing participation
of Democrats in the foreign policy of this country is vital to its
success.

THE DEMOCRATS PUT THEIR FOREIGN-POLICY
MYTH INTO OPERATION

Dean Acheson's uncharacteristically humble remark that "states-
men are not architects but gardeners" holds true most of the
time, but not all of the time. In the practice of diplomacy, there
are architects as well as gardeners. Acheson, who was Truman's
secretary of state during the critical postwar years, was certainly
one of the nation's great architects of its foreign affairs. He
was one of those very few who could imagine something new in
their minds, something practical that could be set firmly in the
reality of the landscape, but that had never existed before. Such
are the people with the plans. These are the architects. Then, to
be sure, there are the gardeners—no less important, but they
are the people who are tending what has already been basically
laid out for them, pruning back unwanted growths or opening
up a side path to help those who need to get where they want to
go, maybe a little more easily. These are the gardeners. In the
landscape of American foreign policy, we have been gardeners
for a lot of the time—we are gardeners now, as a matter of fact—
but the main point is this: when you get right down to it,

only Democrats have been architects in the field of American diplomacy and foreign relations.

There have been but three great paradigms of American foreign policy. They are, first, the Monroe Doctrine, which waved the Europeans off from any further involvement in North America. Second, Manifest Destiny, which thereafter underpinned and justified the full continental expansion of the United States. And third, the idealistic collective security arrangements based in self-determination and human rights born out of the Great War that ended a hundred years ago, a vision that had to wait a further three decades of lost opportunities before we put in place the institutions that were to bring it to reality. We, the Democrats, invented them all. The intellectual and institutional structures we built have defined America's role in the world in time spans counted in generations.

The Monroe Doctrine of 1823 stated that we would refrain from involvement in European power politics, while declaring that any European intervention in the affairs of the entire Western Hemisphere, South as well as North, would be viewed as "dangerous to our peace and safety." As a policy, it sounded evenhanded, but its evenhandedness was merely for show. The United States had no military capacity to enforce the Monroe Doctrine. To assert otherwise is laughable. We had no ability whatsoever to affect European power politics, and we did not even have any real wherewithal to keep the Europeans out of our own neighborhood, either, as the English had demonstrated to us less than a decade earlier, and quite vividly, too, leaving our capital city in ashes.

We had thus made a unilateral public declaration that we could not back up, and therefore we needed a solution for this problem. It was the subtle and economical mind of John Quincy

Adams, James Monroe's secretary of state, that provided the conceptual answer. In Adams's view, we would not make an awkward and formal alliance with the bitterly unpopular English to prevent the Spanish monarchy from returning to South America, as the British Foreign Ministry had suggested to us in the first place (for the original impetus for the idea of the Monroe Doctrine came from London, not Washington). Instead, Adams suggested a unilateral declaration from the Americans warning the Europeans to stay away. The British did not press their original suggestion because they were in the mood to cooperate quietly with us, given that our mutual interests in South America converged at the time, and given all the difficulties caused by the recent War of 1812. The two countries settled into an implicit live-and-let-live relationship. Thus it was that the Monroe Doctrine relied on the British fleet to enforce its anticolonial policy—note the irony. In effect, the United States tacitly accepted the primacy of English power in the Atlantic in order to pursue its own ends on the North American landmass, shielded from distraction and unwelcome European poaching behind the Union Jack of British naval supremacy.

The idealism of the Monroe Doctrine lay in its anticolonialism and its support for the free development of all the republics of the Americas, South as well as North. But for us, the underlying meaning of the Monroe Doctrine was the fate of North America, not South America. Beneath the proudly stated republican idealism of the doctrine, the United States was engaged in a deadly serious maneuver of power politics designed to shrink the boundaries of our foreign-policy interests, narrowing them down to encompass the only area in which we were capable of bringing real power to bear, where we held the advantage rather than the disadvantage—and finally, where we had the most crit-

ical tangible stake: high idealism and raw self-interest. The policy of James Monroe and the man who refined its conceptualization,
Secretary of State John Quincy Adams, held until World War
I and the decline of British arms, when America had to assert
itself in the North Atlantic and throw its weight into the power
balance of Europe itself. Until then, the Monroe Doctrine served
the United States quite well.

And it was the Democratic Party that led America across the
continent, often in the teeth of opposition from the Federalists
and Whigs. Every schoolchild knows the story of President Jefferson's purchase of the Louisiana territory. To this day, his action in 1803 remains the masterstroke of our entire diplomatic
history. The New England Federalists in the Senate, obtusely,
voted against its completion. This pattern was to continue. The
chief characteristic of the Democratic Party's foreign policy
during the 1800s was continental expansionism. In the way the
world worked in that far-off time, we had to acquire the western lands from other nation-states that claimed them—a job
for the State Department and the War Department. It was
the Democratic Party that accomplished almost all of this
acquisition.

Besides Jefferson, the critical figure in this story is the stunning, but somehow inexplicably and inexcusably overlooked,
James K. Polk, the political avatar of Manifest Destiny, a policy
inextricably linked to the larger historical purposes of our party.
The truth is that Polk became one of the most effective presidents
ever to serve the nation, without question our most underrated
chief executive. He concentrated his mind and his energy on the
big things—the things that mattered. He did not allow himself
to be distracted by the secondary things.

He wanted to settle the Oregon question with the British.

He wanted California from the Mexicans. He got them both, plus everything in between as well. Thus, by early 1848, he had brought in the entire continent west of the Louisiana Purchase (except for the Gadsden Purchase along the border with Mexico, arranged by the expansionist Democrat Franklin Pierce six years later). Polk's achievement was every bit the equal of Jefferson's original expansion and, indeed, in some ways even greater, because of the audacity of his conception, the nerve of his maneuver, and the forces, domestic as well as foreign, arrayed against him. He willed his successes into existence and he accomplished them all in a matter of months.

James Polk was a fanatic—grim, humorless, narrow-minded, politically paranoid, partisan in the extreme. The Whigs detested him, and he returned the favor by labeling them traitors. Led yet again by the slippery Henry Clay in the campaign against Polk in 1844, the Whigs went from fearful ambiguities to outright opposition to war with Mexico. After they took control of the House in the 1846 congressional off-year elections, they passed a resolution stating bluntly that the Mexican-American War had been "unnecessarily and unconstitutionally begun by the President of the United States." They opposed the acquisition of any Mexican soil at the war's conclusion. "No territory" was the officially pronounced policy of the Whigs. But the emotional and logical imperative of Manifest Destiny proved politically irresistible. In their brash mood, Americans simply brushed aside the quibblings of Whiggery, and Polk pushed on.

If ever there was a clear example of how to operate a high politics with a low one, both at the same time, Manifest Destiny has got to stand first in line. It was the American analogue of the idealistic, emotional, and romantic European revolutions of the 1848 period. Its high, idealistic face lay in the vision of an

Empire for Liberty from sea to shining sea, and its low face amounted to little more than a land grab. Despite the arguments about all this that can be raised—indeed, are raised, and perhaps with some merit, even today—it is unimaginable what our country might be like right now had Polk and the Democrats not prevailed: the United States without the West.

Manifest Destiny was no mere grand gesture of imperialistic hubris; it was the necessary precondition to adding more states into the American Union. When the underlying sea-to-sea rationale for Manifest Destiny evaporated into success, so, too, did the Democrats' appetite for expansion. Cleveland and Bryan were both proud anti-imperialists, fighting fierce battles against Republicans on this point. The Democrats, for instance, campaigned on the slogan "Republic, Not Empire" during the 1900 Bryan-McKinley contest, when the GOP wanted to take the Philippines as an American colony.

Harry Truman was the last American leader who succeeded in establishing a sustained political framework for the discussion of how America should play out its role in world affairs. But Truman did not invent a new foreign-policy paradigm. Instead, in the 1945–1949 period, he brought to reality the political myth that had been invented by the generous mind of Woodrow Wilson. In the freedoms of the Fourteen Points, with its concepts of self-determination, which aligned us with the aspirations of rising peoples in many parts of the globe, Wilson had seen the possibilities a generation before and set them out before his countrymen, only to fail tragically and nobly in the League of Nations fight of 1919.

After the Second World War, it was the Man from Missouri who was able to make from these ideas a new world, and a new place for America in that world, and Truman reshaped the understanding of the American mind about that place. With the commitment to collective security that FDR had prepared the American people for, and with the founding of the United Nations and the great family of multilateral international institutions, and with programs like the Marshall Plan and NATO, Truman began to implement a framework that embodied American idealism, democratic self-expression, and generosity on the one hand, with a hard-bitten, realistic commitment to containment of the Soviet military, philosophical, and economic challenge on the other.

By and large, it worked. America prospered. And in the idealism and stability of the order that the American people largely underwrote, there flourished a great flowering of freedom and an amazing expansion of economic well-being among other peoples around the globe. Truman's was a triumph of the first order. The paradigm that Truman impressed on the domestic American political conversation about the foreign relations of this country lasted for over a half-century. And the truth is that to an enormous extent, we still live in Truman's world and within the institutions he brought to flower. We work in his garden. Yet today the Truman framework is faltering, and so we are confronted with a new duty: to interpret and improve the world we find ourselves in right now, which is different from Harry Truman's world.

THE DEMOCRATS DROP THE BALL

The contrast between what happened in 1945 and what happened in 1989 could not be sharper. A new age began in 1989. When the Berlin Wall came down and the Communists left the stage, they necessarily took Truman's policy of containment with them. The world itself was therefore suddenly new, but the political mind to encompass that world and to explain it to America was absent. There was only foolish sloganeering about "the world's only superpower" and "the indispensable nation." Catchphrases, to no particular purpose or end. Despite an abruptly different structure of the world community, this time—unlike 1945—there was no new and serious foreign-policy paradigm for the American citizenry to consider and act upon. Here was a major failure of political imagination, and it was to have big consequences.

Of course, this is a national problem, and there is more than enough blame to go around, but some good measure of the onus must fall on the Democrats. Every time in the past, we have been the ones to step forward to suggest the approach that worked: the explanation, the raison d'être for the American role—understandable and sustainable. This time, we have not. Which is tragic. We seem to lack the boldness of our political ancestors.

Having neglected the Party's public duty to construct a credible, coherent international narrative in the period after 1989— and, indeed by neglecting the Party's own self-interest in setting the terms of the foreign-policy discussion—we in effect left it open to our opponents in the George W. Bush administration to suggest a new organizing principle for American foreign policy. When the trauma came with the attack on the country in September 2001, the Republicans were in power, and they were able to feed those terrible events into a new mythical paradigm that empowered them to conduct a different national conversation, not only about foreign policy, but occasionally about domestic policy as well. Their paradigm is the war on terror. Because of its own intellectual and operational flaws, this terror paradigm is not likely to last, but while it does last, its political power to organize the foreign-policy debate is intense and pretty much all-encompassing.

The current tacit acceptance of the Bush foreign-policy paradigm by the Democrats has placed us in a psychological trap that, so far, we have proved powerless to break. We seem frozen in a political crouch, afraid to question, afraid to speak our minds bluntly, afraid to move, and therefore unable to do enough to help the country. America desperately needs a new explanation for our engagement with the outside world. Of course we need to make it clear that we will act to protect our country and our people, but we also need to change the underlying political paradigm that dominates the current foreign-affairs debate. The long-range national interest demands it. For this job, we must repair to our own traditions rather than following George W. Bush's lead.

We live today in a time very much like 1945, an age receptive to invention and new ideas because many of the old ideas and organizing concepts are fading away, withered by the struggle to survive in a world they were never made for. In short, at this particular time and place, Democrats must revert to the critical service we have always performed for the nation: we must become, in foreign affairs, once again, the creative architects for the new age.

We lost the election of 2016, and so we are not in power now, and not operating American foreign policy. We cannot, therefore, govern our way to a new foreign-policy paradigm. But being out of power means that we are more at liberty to think and discuss our way to a new framework for America's involvement with the world—if only we are honest and serious with ourselves and with our compatriots whose allegiance we seek. Time out of power is too valuable to fritter away; it is often the most fertile period of politics. We must use it now.

THINKING AHEAD TO RECOVER OUR
STEP ABROAD

How can our traditions as Democrats help us frame a politics in the world that is responsible to our compatriots at home while advancing American ideals for ourselves and for those outside our borders?

Reinterpret and reassert American idealism. Democrats have insisted on a strong strain of American idealism in our foreign policy because it sets our behavior off from the actions of other great powers. An idealistic foreign policy draws others to us. It translates into real, tangible, and useful power for the United States overseas, legitimizing a whole range of our other interests. It is the emotional political fuel that can sustain the sacrifices the American people have to make for their government's policies abroad. And this sense of potential, this hope for a better life, this belief in a better world, and this support for more respect and more equality among peoples and persons provides Americans with something more than the opportunity to help others abroad. It can free us up from our own narrowness, and the trap of dwelling inordinately on the perils and foreboding of outside menace.

Most importantly, these qualities of idealism represent who we are as a people. By now, the world almost expects this courageous and optimistic view from us. It is therefore reasonable that we should express our own true nature through our foreign policy, just as other nations express theirs. Woodrow Wilson understood that the best approach is to see our ideals firmly and publicly implanted in our foreign policy and have the discussion revolve around questions of common sense concerning how to advance them, and how to update them, given whatever changing context is at hand.

If all of this seems easy enough to say, it turns out to be very difficult to put into practice. There are other important and competing goals to serve in foreign policy demanding the attention and treasure of the United States, and it is often easiest to give our idealisms short shrift. Wilsonian idealism can be dangerous, too, because it can slip from its homeport moorings and drift toward the shoals of hubris and overreach, mesmerized by its own internationalism. Yet without service to these idealistic motivating universal principles, the meaning, vigor, and endurance of American leadership abroad are placed at serious risk.

Anchor action in tangible national interest. These days we seem bereft of practical, rough-and-ready principles to show us where we should rightly act and where we should refrain from acting in foreign policy. Insult, defiance, cruel and sadistic deeds that flout our values—these things, by themselves, present treacherously soft grounds for action. In the absence of lawfully binding treaty obligations, just because we are under pressure to act, even if the pressure is from a friend, is not a sufficient reason for us to commit ourselves. We must insist on more. Where, when, how, and how forcefully America should act abroad should be decided only after the most judicious and clear-eyed assessment of what America's tangible national interests require. National self-interest is entirely legitimate and it deserves the most thoroughgoing, objective, and courageous consideration, instead of the slapdash, emotional, checkbox endorsement it sometimes receives when foreign interventions are under discussion.

Democrats over the years have been internationalists because we are nationalists—nationalists in the sense of being interested in advancing the well-being of all our compatriots who live in this country. We are not stay-at-homers; we do not have an isolationist Little America policy. Our party has endorsed involvement in the world, not shrunk from it. We have been the organizers of this effort, not its disrupters from the outside. We have stood for engagement abroad because we wish to strengthen ourselves at home. The utterly serious James K. Polk had a clear idea in his mind of what our national interest was: before his administration even began, he sat down with his new ambassador to Britain and explained exactly where he was going and what his endgame was. He would settle the Oregon question, by diplomacy and bluff, if possible, and he would take California from Mexico, by force, if necessary, and he brought his expansionist policy to a brilliant and ruthless conclusion.

There are some Democrats today who seem skeptical about applying the yardstick of American interest to our foreign relations. They may see the national interest as narrow or even selfish. They emphasize only the benefits of multilateral internationalist cooperation on issues that transcend national frontiers. They are skeptical about overconfident American adventurism abroad. But questions of American self-interest are the true terms of engagement if Democrats wish to influence the outcome of foreign-policy debates at home. What's in it for us is a completely reasonable and justifiable question for the American people to ask. The usefulness of national self-interest in sorting out foreign-policy priorities and claims depends entirely on how seriously we take it. It is a very flexible tool. Tangible national interest can be a restraining influence on our idealism and our appetite for military action abroad, as well as an expansive one.

Avoid distraction. The road to decline runs through distraction. We don't have unlimited resources these days, and the lives of our young men and women are precious. First things first, and that means the future first, even if the inflammatory drama of the moment threatens to tempt us away. It takes discipline to keep a serious focus on the things that matter most to us, such as the coherence of our alliances, the rules under which we trade with our partners, and our adherence to America's fundamental national ideals.

To conceptualize our problem differently—to imagine, for instance, that we must operate and defend an almost worldwide geographic sphere of influence by ourselves—is to invite the danger of exhausting our treasure and power out on the peripheries of the challenges that are truly critical to us. On July 4, 1821, during the Monroe administration, Secretary of State John Quincy Adams addressed the House of Representatives, commemorating the nation's birthday and suggesting philosophical parameters for U.S. foreign policy. At the time, public pressure was mounting to fever pitch in favor of two foreign entanglements. Americans were demanding robust assistance to South American republicans who were trying to throw off the Spanish monarchy, and the same policy to back Greek partisans who were trying to throw off Ottoman rule.

Adams demurred. He declaimed of our country that "wherever the standard of freedom and Independence has been or shall be unfurled, there will her heart, her benedictions and her prayers be. But she goes not abroad, in search of monsters to destroy. She is the well-wisher to the freedom and independence of all.

She is the champion and vindicator only of her own." His conception is too crimped for America's world role today, yet it holds lessons for modern-day America—lessons about dissipation of energy and distraction of focus, out to the farthest-flung borderlands, and away from the central underpinnings of American predominance. The fate of the United States will not be decided in some far-off mountain valley, away out at the edges.

Rank-and-file Democrats need to raise tough questions when our leaders try to edge us closer to foreign military interventions in places like Grenada, Lebanon, Kuwait, the Balkans, Afghanistan, Iraq, Libya, Yemen, Pakistan, Iran, Syria, the South China Sea, Somalia, the Philippines, Niger, North Korea. Some of those interventions might make sense when measured against the yardstick of our critical long-term national self-interests. Some might not. If we are going in, we need to be tough on our adversaries. If we are considering going in, long before taking the last step, we need to be tough on our own leaders. Do they actually have a clear idea of a long-lasting end result of America's efforts, and a practical and achievable avenue to get there? Will it be worth the cost to us—all kinds of costs?

Be economical. Given the commercial and security realities of our day, America's political leadership needs to find the most economical means of achieving the country's goals, once an apparent consensus on a serious tangible national interest has been achieved. Sometimes it has proved necessary for us to intervene massively to balance a force that was clearly a threat, as with Germany in the first half of the last century. Democrats, with our long record of protecting the national interest by means of unilateral U.S. military force, need to make our preparedness for by-ourselves action clear to our compatriots at home as well as to our potential enemies abroad. On the other hand, some threats might not have been so dire to the United States that we had to intervene so forcefully and expensively as we did. From time to time, we have expended massive amounts of blood and treasure when alternative means might have been better suited to achieving our national purposes.

Here, we need to remind ourselves of the Democratic traditions of expeditious caution, which can be especially useful to remember and act upon in an era like the present one. This is the tradition of John Quincy Adams. We are not operating from a position of perceived weakness in the world now, as he was then. Nevertheless, our resources for dealing with problems like these are more constrained than they seemed to be during the past several generations. Adams's overriding and intensely focused purpose was to help clear the board of foreign powers preparatory to eventual American expansion westward. To achieve his purpose, he could have conducted the obvious and logical foreign policy and backed it up with force. He could have counseled building a huge navy to keep foreigners at bay. He could have counseled militarizing the border with Canada to keep the English out.

But he advised neither of these strategies, and yet he achieved his overall goal. He sheltered American policy in anticolonialist idealism, and arranged for the British to bear the cost of it by maintaining their expensive fleet in the North Atlantic. The tacit live-and-let-live understandings he engineered between the United States and the United Kingdom can still be seen today in the longest demilitarized boundary in the world: between the United States and Canada. Even as he was arranging all this, however, he and the British both knew that he held an implicit threat-card in his pocket: trouble on the border. In defining the national interest so succinctly, and advancing it so efficiently, Adams's exceedingly deft diplomacy provides a lesson in craft for us in our own day.

There is no way, however, that America can perform a leading world role if we continue to succumb to the kind of unhealthy and gloomy defensiveness that has all too often tainted the world view of American leaders since 2001. But the presidential campaign of 2016, stained by so many other deeply disturbing watermarks, offered not much hope to those who might have looked for a reassertion of the made-by-Democrats traditionally dominant framework for American foreign policy. And after our defeat, when we were out and should have been looking hard at a world that was changing dramatically, and changing fast—the muscular assertiveness of China, the new boldness of Russia's outward push, the rise of old nationalisms that called into question the viability of the liberal European experiment that had held sway for three-quarters of a century—there was no serious second look at where we were in the world, and where we needed to go. There was no serious searching of ourselves as Democrats either, and how we might make sense of the new world we found ourselves in, or how we might seek to explain it to ourselves and our countrymen by updating the intellectual framework that we ourselves had originally invented. We are being overtaken by events.

The underlying foreign-policy paradigm is what now needs to be reconsidered. For this task—which, again, is like the other jobs of deep politics, that is, a challenge in ideas and ideals—Democrats must look to Wilson, FDR, and Truman, the three great American internationalists of the twentieth century, who exuded self-assurance about our country and its people. The genius of the American politicians, diplomats, and military officers who constructed the present system of international institutions during the postwar period rested in their seriousness, their self-confidence, and their generosity. What made their work last was their determination to imprint it with the finest face of American idealism. America as Redeemer Nation was in it, not as a madcap adventure of national hubris, but as a standard of human dignity that others were pleased and grateful to rally round. Qualities like seriousness, self-confidence, and generosity do not give out because you use them. These wellsprings remain, even in times when spirits are low. They are the critical component for America's work of international agenda-setting in the immediate future.

To suggest that our political leaders are incapable of doing what Truman did, of constructing a forceful argument in support of making a new world, is to imply that the current Democratic leadership is utterly devoid of political imagination. It would be even more grotesque to imply that the American citizenry is now incapable of demonstrating the seriousness to support such an argument based in idealism and self-interest.

Neither proposition is plausible.

7

ALL MEN ARE CREATED EQUAL

Lyndon Johnson and Civil Rights

All men are created equal: a vital founding political myth of the Democrats. After so much trouble and bad faith, Jefferson's great principle led us, finally, to our modern commitment to civil rights. The mission of the Democratic Party in America is to strengthen and stabilize the Republic in justice by recognizing and embedding new communities within the national mainstream.

March 15, 1965: A night of high politics—high politics truly of the first order. It was perhaps the only act of high politics by an elected official on the national stage during the lifespan of any modern generation of Americans. It was high politics because there was high principle behind it, and it was filled with personal agony. It captured, in a single public moment, a tectonic shift of political forces. It was real; there was nothing cosmetic about it, and the changes it would bring would make all the difference. Finally, it was high politics because it was incontrovertibly and

irretrievably a deliberate and intentional act against the immediate self-interest of a political party. Such a thing almost never
happens in politics. It was the last hour of the mighty southern
wing of the Democratic Party.

A NIGHT OF HIGH POLITICS

Enforcement of the citizen's right to cast a ballot was the issue.
The president was Lyndon Johnson. He stood in the well of the
House that night before a joint session of Congress, and spoke to
the People about the values and meaning of America. From his
very first words, you knew it was going to be serious: "I speak to-
night for the dignity of man and the destiny of Democracy." He
maintained that we were the first nation in the history of the
world founded with a purpose: "The great phrases of that purpose still sound in every American heart, North and South: 'All
men are created equal.'" The job of the government was "to right
wrong, to do justice, to serve man." He reminded the members
of Congress that they had sworn an oath to protect and defend
the Constitution, and he told them that they now had to act in
obedience to that oath. He laid it down bluntly, denying that
there was any moral issue before them in the Congress, because
what they had been doing all along was wrong. Promises had
been made, and they had gone unkept. "We have already waited
a hundred years and more and the time for waiting is gone," he
told them. And then, as if proclaiming the crack of doom, he put
it to them starkly: "The time of justice has now come." Over and
over, the president fused the purposes of the federal government
to those of the insurgent civil rights movement; deliberately,
slowly, he repeated the words again and again throughout his

speech: "*We shall overcome.*" The speech was a thunderclap in the middle of the civil rights struggle—the closest thing to a revolution the nation had experienced since the Civil War.

He was introducing the Voting Rights Act, which would change not only the South, but ultimately the whole nation. Though but a pedestrian speechmaker, Lyndon Johnson pulled out all the stops that night. The inspiring words of his speech can still bring forth tears. He was personal. He talked of his own roots going deep into southern soil. He reminded the nation of the military sacrifices the South had made for the Republic, the honor and gallantry of its soldiers. He invoked—how could he not?—the name of Abraham Lincoln, "a great president of another party." It was remarkable that a man like Lyndon Johnson could have been the one to make a speech like this, but it was, in important ways, amazing that his political party should have been the one to put itself behind his words. It was a riveting moment in the history of the nation.

Much of the drama of the occasion was offstage. President Johnson was standing athwart history. He was in the present, but the past was all about him. He stood amidst the history of the nation, but even more specifically, he stood athwart the terrible history of his political party, not to mention the history of his own personal political career and his own complicity in it all. The visible stage may have been the well of The People's House, but the unseen stage was a backdrop stained with the original sin of the president's own political party, the Democratic Party— North as well as South. Your party and mine.

The gathering of the Party's ghosts gave the president's speech much of its impact: Thomas Jefferson, dreading "the fire bell in the night," but not freeing his slaves; Andrew Jackson, setting up the removal of American Indians onto the Trail of Tears; the aggressively obtuse Franklin Pierce—ours; the feckless James Buchanan—ours again; the religious William Jennings Bryan, conniving with white supremacists and apologizing for the Klan; the high-minded Woodrow Wilson, politely signing a law to reimpose racial segregation on integrated workplaces of the federal government; FDR, turning a deaf ear to his wife's pleas to back legislation making lynching a federal crime, in order to maintain his political arrangements; and even the ever-cautious JFK. They were all there. They had all benefited from the moral corruption of our past.

THE RACIAL BARGAIN OF THE DEMOCRATS FOR WHITE SUPREMACY—AND HOW WE CHANGED

For today's Democrats, there is no way around this essential shame: our party was the political party of the white man in nineteenth-century America, to the exclusion of all others, and it remained the party of whites in the South for most of the twentieth century, too. In no way was this a gentlemen's agreement. It was flatly stated by the Democrats, up front, in public, for all to see and recognize. "White Supremacy" remained in the official motto of the Democratic Party of Alabama until 1966. This racial bargain for white supremacy sealed the emotional loyalty of the Democrats who flocked to the polls for us, especially, but not only, in the South. The Party was built on it in the South, and the national party depended on it to maintain its power on Capitol Hill and its occasional grip on the White House. Democrats were afraid to take on the implications of our racial bargain, for the very reason that we did depend on it. We remained afraid for over a century and a half. And then we changed.

On that March night in 1965, Lyndon Johnson brought his party face-to-face with the job of dismantling the modern social structure of the old southern and Border States. How could this be? How could it have been a Democrat who did this, and not a Republican? It should seem to have been in the political interest of the Republicans to destroy the lock the Democrats had on the South by carrying forward the logic of what they still called, in those now long-gone days, the Party of Lincoln. But instead, it was the Democrats themselves who did it. And the reason for this goes well beyond the shattering political pressures that so justifiably erupted in the 1960s.

The reason can be found in something clean and true and clear that runs beneath the lurid history of the Democratic Party, with its sordid racial bargains designed to keep us in power for all those long years. The reason is the originating myth of the Democratic Party. It is Jefferson's myth again—always, somehow, we repair to Jefferson—and on this question, once again, he provides the intellectual framework of the Democrats. This is the myth that we have always understood instinctively, no matter how often we have averted our gaze. All the Democrats' political calculations militated in favor of maintaining our racial bargain. Only our myth opposed it. That was the meaning of President Johnson's speech of March 15, 1965. We Democrats— finally—were returning to our originating myth as articulated by Thomas Jefferson: "All men are created equal." We chose the political myth over the political calculation. We faced up to what had to be faced up to. We confronted ourselves.

President Johnson's political action that night produced a reaction that was physical. The moment the president began to speak you could see it begin to unfold, right there in the chamber. Because along with the Party's ghosts, the living were there, too, the white southern Democratic congressmen and senators who, like Johnson himself in Texas, operated the segregated South. They sat and listened to him, frozen rigidly in their seats as the chamber erupted in cheers. In the space of half an hour, the southerners watched Lyndon Johnson turn on their collective history together, and turn on them personally, his friends of a lifetime.

And over the next decade, in all the little towns and in the big cities and along the country roads throughout the old South, there was a turning away from the Democratic Party by white people. For part of that time, I was Secretary of the Democratic Party of Virginia, and the stops along the campaign trail stay with me still, even today; I remember telling people what I did in politics and watching them turn aside from me, firmly, quietly, formally—physically—in unmistakable retaliation. And it was fair enough, I suppose. I believed with all my heart in what the Party was doing, and I was actively advancing it. They were falling to the other side, abandoning us for the suddenly safe Republicans.

The physical shock of it retarded a Democratic response, and I wonder why, even now, there doesn't appear to be a more assured, self-confident Democratic story line—a nonracial narrative—to recover the loyalty of white southerners. Whites in the Deep South have recently voted Republican by margins of as high as three-to-one. Lyndon Johnson understood what he was doing that night in the spring of 1965; he said it at the time in private, that he knew he was delivering the South to his opponents for a whole generation.

Yet it has now been almost two generations, and the prevailing pattern of votes hasn't shifted much. It will do us no good to rest easy in the statistical columns showing that minorities are increasing and whites are decreasing in the national electorate. Grateful and faithful we must be, as we govern the country, to those who support us handsomely, but if we are to remain the Party of The People, we must conceive and promulgate a persuasive and honorable argument that reaches broadly across racial and ethnic barriers, and if we are to continue as a national party, we must figure out how to carry states across all regions of the nation.

THE DEMOCRATIC CITIZEN: WHOLE, COMPLETE, EQUAL

What was it that allowed the Democrats to move so decisively in 1965 from white supremacy into civil rights? For the Democrats, man was whole and complete, meant to stand sufficient unto himself, no more a man, no less a man, than anyone else. There were to be no hierarchies here, as there had been in the Old World. Of course, there were rich and poor men, smart and slow men, but man as political man, in America, could admit no such gradations. His status as citizen stood him in exactly the same stead as the president. One man was not and could not be a "more deserving" or "better" citizen than the next man. It was impossible for a man in struggle or trouble to be "helped" toward a more complete citizenship. There could be no such thing as an interim status, someone who was sort of a citizen, or halfway there. For the Democrat, the idea of encountering a human being who had an ambiguous or marginal status was an absurdity, an act against nature. Hence, the Democratic hostility to the idea of an American colonial subject, or the notion of an "illegal alien." A person was there or he was not. He was in or he was out.

This all-in-or-all-out view created devastating problems because, in the beginning, the African American slave was out. Yet the Democratic irony is that this all-or-nothing philosophy (the same one that blinded us to the evils of slavery in the doomed South and then brought forth its poisoned spawn of segregation out of the ashes) was the very same philosophy that finally impelled us to move our party completely and entirely behind the civil rights uprising. We switched, and no going back, from nothing to all. That same philosophy dictated that, in the critical hour, it should be the Democrats—and not the fiddling and rearguard Republicans, lost in the footnotes of the legislation, feverishly seeking to erect new hierarchies and open special exceptions—who would begin to redeem the nation and the great promise penned by Thomas Jefferson in 1776.

The constitutional texts and advice of our Founding Fathers, so admirable in their rationalism, can make it easy to forget, for a moment, that we are not only a nation of high ideals and abstract ideas; we are also a nation of tribes. All men are created equal is the foundational myth of the Democrats that today involves groups of Americans, blocs of belief and blood. We have almost always been for bringing new blocs of people in; our opponents have almost always been for keeping them out. The terms and the cast of characters of this struggle have changed repeatedly down through the years—from the yeoman farmers of Jefferson's day and the backwoodsmen of Jackson's era running up to today's Democratic demands for equality and dignity for gay Americans—but the essential struggle has not changed. The Democrats who followed Thomas Jefferson believed him when he wrote that all men were created equal. The Jeffersonian credo was clear, and, sometimes despite themselves, it led the Democrats inexorably to bedrock political faith. We fight under the battle standard of including more groups of people in the national community.

This instinct for civil rights, this commitment to fight for the full participation of minorities in American society, with all the rights and responsibilities that go with that participation, is by now deeply ingrained in the Democratic psyche. The Party fully understands the need for this founding Democratic myth. We may have wandered from some of our other pillars of belief, but by this one we stand firm. The core of America is in it. This political ideal, in fact, is so strong among Democrats that it can sometimes seem even to define the essential meaning of today's Democratic Party for millions of Americans. The Party is not going to turn its back on "all men are created equal." Nor need it. Nor should it.

Nevertheless, even with the pride we can justifiably take in our work, honesty compels us to admit that our story hasn't always been quite the heroic saga just laid forth. The African Americans were not the only ones who suffered. Even as the inclusive pattern is undeniably more true than it is untrue, there have been exceptions. Native Americans everywhere, Chinese on the West Coast, and Japanese Americans during the Second World War all felt the icy indifference or sometimes even outright hostility of the Democrats.

One need look no further than the greatest expansion of democratic rights in our country's history: women's suffrage. It was a long struggle, and the women had to carry it forward, more alone than in the company of the nation's political institutions. William Jennings Bryan was an early and consistent supporter of women's voting rights, but other figures, like Wilson, proved more diffident. Even though it might be reassuring to pause and bathe our record in retrospectively rosy-colored hues, the Democrats were not dependable stalwarts in this fight, and therefore women's suffrage is not a particularly good example of Democratic service to Democratic myth. In fact, both major parties tacitly allowed their members to arrive at their own positions individually, even as the women soldiered on alone; party discipline and party courage were conspicuously absent on this question. In retrospect, the ultimate triumph of the women's struggle for suffrage is perhaps rendered all the more noble for having been accomplished largely without institutional assistance.

THE DEMOCRAT AND THE IMMIGRANT

In the mind of the Democrat, all persons were to be made citizens, alike and of equal worth, and soon. Thus, for the Democrats, it made sense to encourage new groups to enter the inner sanctum of American democracy. It made sense philosophically (and, of course, it made sense on Election Day, if you knew what you were doing). The question of immigration, therefore, has always been front-and-center for the Democratic Party, from the very first moment. Imbedded in the notorious Federalist Alien and Sedition Acts of 1798 was the Naturalization Act, and it increased the number of years before immigrants could become eligible for citizenship from five to fourteen. The Naturalization Act was targeted squarely at Irish and French immigrants because they had publicly demonstrated against Federalist measures, and the Federalists logically feared they would vote with the Jeffersonians if they got the ballot. We repealed the Naturalization Act in 1802.

How to handle immigration was at the center of the Democratic calculation in the latter half of the nineteenth century and into the beginning of the twentieth because it went to the very survival of the Party. After the end of reconstruction in 1877, Democratic control of the South was premised on the white man's antipathy for the African American. There was an analogue for the Grand Old Party in the North and the Middle West. Nativism and religion were the fuel that made the Republican machine go, above the Mason-Dixon Line, just as they had been for the Know Nothings before the Civil War. GOP control of areas outside the solid South often rested on the Protestant's animus toward the Catholic and fear of the immigrant, who tended to be, of course, a Roman Catholic. Campaigns for blue laws, plumping for prohibition, antipornography drives to clear out the dirty books, hostility toward parochial schools— these fit nicely with the Republican mantra for purification, a campaign to purify America, as they said. They were all designed to mobilize the Protestant of vigilant rectitude. They were of a piece with the infamous, last-minute slur of the 1884 presidential contest, casting the Democrats as the party of "Rum, Romanism and Rebellion." We can be thankful indeed for Rum and Romanism, at least, since after the Civil War, the Democrats had every reason to fear that the charge of rebellion and treason would stick when the Republicans waved the bloody shirt. It was the immigrants in the North and Midwest who cast the Democrats the line that saved the Party as a national institution.

The nineteenth-century immigrant often mistrusted government, and for good reason, given his experience in Europe; he preferred to rely on personal networks for assistance: the boss at work, the priest in the parish, the native-born cousin. The Democrats' solution to this problem a century and a half ago was the political machine. Our machine was the intermediary between the immigrant and his new government. It offered the immigrant in need a go-to man ready to explain the system, or, better yet, to put the fix in. The machine was constructed to be comprehensible to the new arrival and to prove its worth to him. The political boss needed as many immigrant votes as he could find, and the immigrant needed a friend in power. The logic was incontrovertible. Did the operators of the machine expect to be repaid on Election Day? You bet they did. Was it a corrupt system? Of course it was. But in a rough sort of way, it worked, and the new arrival understood how to make it work for himself.

Bryan got many immigrant votes during his campaigns, but he missed their melody, and he never got enough of their votes to see him through. It was a colossal lost opportunity for the Democrats. The man who did finally jam the two together—the northern cities teeming with immigrants and the farms and small towns of the South and West—was the intellectually embracing Woodrow Wilson. He was able to do it because, unlike Bryan, he worked very hard at doing it, at understanding the immigrant and how he functioned in society. Wilson's speeches about the dignity of immigrants and their special ties to America (because they alone make a voluntary, intentional decision for America) are lyrical paeans to our country and remain emotionally affecting to this day.

LATINOS TODAY: FUSIONISTS IN MYTH

During his Voting Rights Act speech, President Johnson sought to demonstrate his bona fides, his understanding of racial and ethnic prejudice, and to do so, he told a personal story. Interestingly, the story did not concern African Americans or the Deep South, the subjects of his address that night. Instead, it was a story about Mexican Americans. He spoke about his first job out of college, teaching school in the small South Texas town of Cotulla. "My students were poor," he told the members of Congress, "and they often came to class without breakfast and hungry. And they knew even in their youth the pain of prejudice. They never seemed to know why people disliked them, but they knew it was so because I saw it in their eyes. . . . Somehow you never forget what poverty and hatred can do when you see its scars on the hopeful face of a young child."

President Johnson knew Mexican Americans well, and his career in public service amply demonstrated the help he gave them when it suited his overall strategy. The story still has the power to move, and the president told it to emphasize his belief that there were Americans of all ethnic backgrounds, white and brown as well as black, who had reason to claim the scars of unfairness, and that he intended to do something about it.

Johnson's story, which had the note of a regional reminiscence about it fifty years ago, today has national scope. Everyone now recognizes that the story of the Latino community in this country is much broader, much more complicated, and much more critical to the Republic's future than it was half a century ago. What we really have here is the current-day test of the Democrats' professed faith in their Jeffersonian political myth of the equality of man. The mission of the Democratic

Party in America is to strengthen and stabilize the Republic in justice by recognizing and embedding new communities within the national mainstream. Will the Democrats act to bring the Latinos in?

You would think that the Democrats would take on this job as a political imperative of the first order. Already, the Latino community is well over 50 million strong, and by the time today's youth has retired, it will amount to roughly 30 percent of the nation's population. Already, in its massed strength, it has proved it can turn a national presidential election. The population of these communities is not only growing; it is spreading geographically to new parts of the nation, beyond its former strongholds in California, the Southwest, New York, and Chicago. Power is on the move. You would think that trends like these would focus the attention of the Democrats. For some reason, however, the zealotry and sense of social mission our political forebears carried in their breasts a century and a half ago seem lacking today. These days, Democrats take the field tremulously, through Hispanic coordinators in boxes on organization charts.

In the nineteenth century, the numbers of the immigrant community cast our party the lifesaving line that ensured its survival. Remembering our history, Democrats imagined, logically enough, that we were once more faced with a numbers problem: how, mechanically, to capture the lion's share of the new, burgeoning Hispanic vote? This is where, with our first step, we have gone wrong. Because the political problem is not truly about the numbers. It is about the nature of the Latino community, instead of its statistics. The true challenge Democrats need to grapple with is about what kind of people Latinos are and what they believe in and what they have to contribute to the common culture of the United States.

Everyone is struggling now for a way to understand the relationship between Latinos and this country. Anglos who are alert are looking for a useful explanation. Even Latinos are looking for the simple, clarifying narrative arc to explain their story to the country, indeed to explain it to themselves. Of course, the Latinos themselves must conceive this narrative in the first place. Even so, this reality does not exempt political parties from their responsibilities to join in the efforts to arrive at a compelling explanation. This is exactly the kind of business political parties are supposed to be in. They, too, should have something to contribute.

The political party that figures out how to explain this relationship by constructing a clear, emotional, simple story linking Latinos to the United States is likely to have the inner track on achieving the loyalty of these communities far into the future. A narrative of the kind we are talking about here has to be immediately understandable to the community whose story it is trying to explain. Furthermore, it can enjoy no life in a sealed-off compartment. The narrative must be the same, whether it is being told to the mainstream of the nation or to the particular communities it pertains to. It has to cover pretty nearly all the people it professes to explain. The narrative needs a challenge and a resolution. Even as it deals in struggle, it needs to hold the possibility of reaching a dignified resolution, for the community as well as for the country. It cannot offer only division, much less victimization; somehow, the potential for some kind of ultimate unity has to be present. It has to take on the quality of an operable political myth, in other words. Nothing sure and all-encompassing has so far appeared. Here lies political opportunity of enormous scope.

The loyalty of Latinos to the United States is not under question, but their loyalty to the two major political parties is very decidedly split. In a normal election, the GOP garners about a third of the Latino vote. Democrats have lulled themselves into a political lethargy because the margins the Latino community returns them on election night have usually been comfortably satisfactory in recent years and therefore the Democrats keep on keeping on without bothering to look closely enough at the community they are dealing with. Our advantage rests largely in the crude efforts of the Grand Old Party to portray Latinos as communities of people ominously set aside from authentic Americans. As long as the Republicans fail to embrace a reasonable and forward-looking position on comprehensive immigration reform, this lopsided Democratic advantage is likely to persist, especially in the Mexican American community, which is by far the largest. In the wake of the astonishing 2016 election campaign, Republicans are unlikely to make significant gains in these communities, but just imagine what would happen to us if the Republicans were to wake up, move beyond the immigration debate, and make a determined effort to enlist significant majorities of the Latino vote, as they have already done with the white working-class vote. The national calculus could shift.

Latino political ideas do not fit coherently and seamlessly together. Latinos are a study in fertile contradiction, and this is precisely why they should be of particular interest to the Democrats today. The underlying political and economic points of view and temperaments of the people in these communities are difficult to encompass or summarize. In many respects, Latinos are very conservative. They can be traditionalists. They are family-values people, almost without peer. They are the most anti-abortion grouping of any segment of the U.S. population, according to the opinion polls. They follow the flag. They are hard workers. You don't hear people in this community question the value of working to get ahead or making more money to support their families. The rate of private-business formation within the Latino community is double, and by some counts triple, the overall national rate. Latinos in this country are primarily working in the private sector, not in the public or nonprofit sector. They are starting and working in all kinds of businesses, not just mom-and-pop businesses. They are building the country.

Yet while it is manifestly true that millions of Latinos are private-enterprise people driven by individual initiative, who expect government to stay out of the way, at the same time, these are communities that depend heavily on government services and benefits. Beneath today's Latino numerical surge there lies a fascinating series of political problems and philosophical questions.

Latino culture is a dramatic fusion of Spaniards from Europe and indigenous peoples from this hemisphere, rooted centuries in the past. Right from the beginning, Latinos carried a deep understanding for the melding of cultures and the mixture of contradictions. They are good at wending their way through the clash of cultures, because they have had to be good at it. Furthermore, as a community, they have arrived at the fulcrum of the political conversation in the United States at precisely the moment when all Americans are beginning to understand that the old assimilation paradigm for past immigrations is shifting in significant ways. The ethnic questions of this country can no longer be understood simply as new groups trying to figure out how to fit in with the dominant Anglo culture, and the Anglos trying to figure out how to accommodate the newcomers. The idea of just pasting new groups onto the skin of the American body politic has been eclipsed by a new reality.

A genuinely polyglot America must now figure out what the meaning of the nation might be in the future. To take a consequential hand in this job, Democrats need to gather a wide range of serious and substantive ideas from all kinds of Americans, something much more than just a rainbow of ethnicities or a list of detailed policy options. The Latinos bring something new, different, and distinct, something of their own that they are in a position to offer up. And, indeed, those Latinos who have immigrated here are, almost by definition, people who embrace not only the United States, but also the idea of change, and this means that they are in a mood to contribute to the changes that are shaping our common emerging political culture.

The root of the national Democratic political problem is to understand how to encompass two contradictory poles of its own intellectual heritage: the pole of energetic individual responsibility and initiative and the pole of communal responsibility for those who need a helping hand up. This is the new dialogue the Democratic Party needs to have with itself. The Latino community understands both these poles simultaneously. It needs to interject itself aggressively into this Democratic debate. The Democratic Party needs to pay close attention to the ideas and ideals of the Latino community, instead of just counting the numbers. The Latino community has consequential lessons in philosophy and temperament to teach modern Democrats.

THE FIGHT FOR THE LATINOS AND THE MYTH
OF ECONOMIC OPPORTUNITY

The ultimate partisan loyalty of the Latino community in the United States, as between our two national parties, may be decided on grounds that have less to do with ethnicity than many of today's practicing Democratic politicians suppose. Ethnicity will retain its own importance, but other factors may be more important. The loyalty of Latinos to this nation is fundamentally based in the concept of opportunity. The break, the prospect for getting ahead—this is where the political battle for the ultimate loyalty of Latinos is likely to take place. Latinos are workers looking for the main chance. The Democrats have not spoken sufficiently to the phenomenal Latino appetite to flourish as an operator of private enterprise.

This is inexplicable for a party with its roots in the private, as opposed to the public, economy. If you search carefully through the political problem of Latinos in America today, you can discover some echoes of the original moving spirit of the Democratic Party. The Latino community today is filled with individual economic strivers, and this is precisely where the Democrats began two centuries ago, in emphatic service to the individual and a commitment to clearing a path for his advancement. As the country grew more complicated and its economic power became more concentrated over the years, we turned our attention to questions of bigness and all the problems bigness posed. But in our new focus, Democrats sometimes lost hold of our first focus. Our first focus was on the individual, the little guy who wanted to start a little business and work on it and see if he could make it grow. Most of the American economy today is based on the efforts of people just like these. Millions and millions of Americans work in these businesses.

Sometimes these days, we Democrats can feel that we are at a disadvantage in this part of the economic argument. The idea of America as the land of economic opportunity really originated with the Whigs and not with the Democrats. The Republicans today preach the old America-is-a-hierarchy Whig myth to the nation in general and to the Latinos in particular, and it has a natural way of falling from their lips. Today's Republican story, like the Whig myth of the self-made man, is one of economic advancement for the self: you can make it here; you can make it by relying on yourself; you can climb the ladder, rung by rung, from one perch to the next; don't worry about the rules of the game; you shouldn't rely on the government; you don't need to; this is America; it's the land of opportunity. This is a particularly powerful message in the Latino community, and the Democratic Party would do very well to listen to it more closely than it has in recent years. It is an argument made by the GOP directly to the individual Latino voter, as an individual, concerning individual behavior. It establishes a straight-line, direct link between the Republican Party and the single citizen. It is tough and clear. It is having an effect.

Hard work, bootstrapping, individual initiative: What American is going to step out of line to quarrel publicly with traits like these? They are traits widely prevalent in all the various Latino communities, not just one or two, and they therefore unite those communities with each other rather than divide them from each other. They are traits that all Americans, of any ethnicity or belief, have a basic respect for, and any fair-minded American, watching Latinos at work in this country, will agree, either grudgingly or willingly, that these qualities are on full display among Hispanics. This economic-opportunity narrative of the Republicans, as they preach it to the Latino community, is about similarity, not about difference. It is therefore a unifying myth of national scope, not a divisive one.

Yet the Democrats need to pick a new fight with the Republicans over this raft of issues. We have our own distinct political and intellectual roots, and we have every reason to be self-confident about them. Our ideals are different from the ideals of the Whigs and the Republicans. The old Whig economic myths are certainly still relevant—and we should feel free to poach from them—but some of our ideals might well be more relevant to individual Latinos today. We are the ones who are for the little guy. We are for the outsider. Here, in our own Democratic traditions of economic justice, is the energetic, get-ahead, go-ahead striver. This is the American whom Jackson sought to unleash and for whom Wilson cleared the way.

Emphatically, we are the ones who show the determination to change the rules of the game so that the little guy can get ahead. We are not let-alone people when it comes to the rules of the economic struggle. We also believe that the government should be there to lend a hand to the outsider. We started the Small Business Administration during the Depression. The Republicans have been trying to kill and defund it ever since. We should put it front-and-center again, and pour more money into it. As Democrats, we should play to our own advantage. We are ahead of the game with Latinos now. We should solidify our position for when the immigration fights are over.

Americans of all ethnicities who are struggling with the unfair rigidities of society's rules understand and endorse and respect a politics that enlists with determination in the Fight for the Outsider. The same ideals that work for black and brown outsiders are key to bringing back to our fold those Americans who have fallen away from us during the last half-century, most definitely including the white working class. This is the way forward for Democrats now: to speak to the common problems of the Common Man.

At their most profound, these are civil rights issues. The lesson for today's Democratic politics: Democrats need to think about these issues in ways that will bring various ethnic communities into alliance with each other, instead of segregating them into their own special stand-alone categories. Repeatedly, when Lyndon Johnson delivered his voting rights message to Congress in March 1965, this was what he emphasized. He was presenting them with a civil rights bill whose object was to ensure that African American citizens could exercise their right to vote, "but in a larger sense," he said, "its object is to open the city of hope to all people of all races."

THE NEW DEMOCRACY

It was commonly said, in the wake of the 2016 election, that no one could remember what, if anything, the Democrats had stood for during the campaign. And, in fact, we had ignored the larger American context of our own policies. In leaving the most important part of the fight alone, we created a political vacuum. The Republican Party filled that vacuum. That's the way they brought us down. In reality, we were the ones who set ourselves up for it, before the contest even began.

But this criticism is more interesting as it pertains to the general state of the Democratic Party at the current time than as a comment on the past performance of any one candidate. For it is the intellectual traditions of the Democratic Party that are in trouble these days, and these go deeper and remain longer than a single candidacy. They are what, in the first instance, require renewed attention now. The current disrepair of parts of the Democratic credo—and how to work them back in with other elements of the Party's legacy of ideals—presents Democrats with problems in the politics of political myth that are practical—

practical in the sense that their festering blocks our ability to win elections, but practical also because these are problems that we ourselves can fix.

THE NEW DAY

Democrats have lost control of the national political conversation, and the reason is that we have lost control over the fundamental terms that underpin the debate. This is the elemental problem for the Democratic Party today, and it has persisted, and intensified, through decades and cycles of elections.

We lost control of the domestic-politics argument in 1980 when Ronald Reagan got elected by imposing his lesser/least-is-always-best philosophy of government on the national discussion, replacing FDR's New Deal economic-security ideal. We lost control of the foreign-policy debate after September 2001, when George W. Bush imposed his terror lens, eclipsing the outward-looking and optimistic ideals and interests framework the Democrats had championed since 1823. We never bothered even to try to recover from either of these two political body blows. When 2016 arrived, it brought a Republican candidate for president who organized his politics around root purpose, anchoring it in simple, emotional paradigms. He won his election, and the key to his success lay in broadening the coalition of constituencies in the Grand Old Party. He accomplished that by expanding the ideals beyond those that the GOP had traditionally stood for. Some of those ideals—ignominiously for Democrats—he purloined from the long legacy of the Democratic Party in American history, twisting their meanings, but succeeding, nevertheless, in robbing us of the massive support we once earned from working-class voters. A one-two-three punch in the arena of political paradigms. No wonder we have felt beset from all sides since Ronald Reagan's election in 1980. No wonder we feel even more beset after the 2016 election.

In the power struggle, when you lose control of the big terms of reference that lie behind the daily details, you have already lost the political argument. Then, it's not only much harder for you to get elected, but even if you do manage to get elected, you're always playing catch-up as you try to govern, because you're playing on your opponents' turf: they have set the rules of the game, and you are maneuvering narrowly between the sidelines of their basic ideas, not yours. Essentially, the Democrats are still playing on Ronald Reagan's field today, using his rules. And George W. Bush and Donald Trump have piled on, adding their playbook of ideals to his.

There is really only one question in politics, and that is "What is the question?" What is the fundamental question in the campaign that turns a majority of the votes? Change the underlying question, and you change the result.

Democrats can escape the political downdraft we are caught in. We can do that by recovering our presence of mind. We can do it by reasserting the mind of the Democratic Party itself. This is the path back to power for the Democrats. It lies open before us. The cornerstones of a new Democratic politics rest in the seven political myths of our own heritage, the defining beliefs of our own tradition. We can restore our health by reclaiming our soul.

Thus, in truth, despite the shock and occasional despair, there is real hope for those floundering in the wake of the Republican sweep of 2016. If the Democrats have been late in facing up to an honest and serious reassessment of their meanings for America, their own root purposes for being in politics in the first place, they are not too late. If the year following the Trump election proved inconclusive, the years moving forward will prove decisive for a redefinition of Democratic purpose, and, indeed, for the future shape and fault lines of American politics at large. The big, fork-in-the-road, fundamental choices before the Democratic Party have become clearer, and more insistently unavoidable. What kind of party are we to make for ourselves, and for the country at large, looking forward? This is the discussion the Democratic Party can no longer postpone.

It is the larger political life of the nation that has forced the hand of the Democrats. It offered up to the Democrats many more concrete opportunities to thrash out the future of their party than they had been able to see right after the 2016 election. The next two years, the next three years—now is our time. Now is the New Day.

For now, the rebuilding of the local base of the Party will begin in earnest, and who will local organizers seek to bring in? Will they show the courage to find and welcome new kinds of Democrats, and old Democrats who have fallen away, in addition to the tried-and-true? And those Democrats who are already inside the Party, who had got used to the comfortable old party that existed before November 2016, will they accept the newcomers and home-comers, and open their hearts to them, and make a respectful place for them to state their case inside the Party? Candidates are venturing into races for offices far down the ballot, long since lost to the knowledge or even interest of the Party's sophisticated leaders and consultants. Local Democratic committees are reorganizing; the people who get themselves elected to these committees in their home precincts *are* the Democratic Party. How will they exert their power? How will they exercise their influence over officeholders and candidates? The debates will come—the chance to test our ideas before the public, and to feel immediately in the room whether we are connecting or not. Our own primaries, which are by design open to anyone with a courageous determination who wants to run and has something to say and decides to take a hand in molding the future of the new Democratic Party, will be on tap. Then will come the chaotic, high-stakes conventions, which can demand the instant decisions that tell you whether someone has political judgment or not. Then the campaigns, which pour on the pressure out in the open, month after month, denying a sanctuary of secrecy to the candidate with nothing to say or something to hide. The temporary clarity that the next cycle of general elections will provide in 2018—and then, critically of course, the long run-up to our presidential nomination in 2020, with its big divisions and its search for a new coherence. And even beyond, into the legislative redistricting that determines the kinds of communities where the destiny of the country will be decided.

For all of us, all of this is the chance to communicate something serious to our compatriots—*our own ideals*, not exactly as Jefferson or Jackson or Bryan or Wilson or FDR understood them—of course not—but rather as we ourselves understand them right now, in the light of our own experience in today's world. These ideals are the pillars of creed that can serve as practical and optimistic bearings for the future of a worried nation. Our job now is to bring new faith out of old wisdom. If we prove worthy of that job, our fellow citizens will bring us back to power.

But the Democrats will have to adjust their focus in order to put themselves in the position to seize these opportunities. They will have to begin by focusing on themselves.

The New Conversation will settle the question of who the Democrats really are.

THE NEW CONVERSATION

Who is going to win out in this new conversation about what the Democratic Party will look like in the future? Who is going to come out on top, and what are the best strategies for prevailing in the battles that now loom before us? These are the questions that tacticians for outside pressure groups, special-interest lobbyists, and the Party's consultants want answers to. That's understandable. They reflect the temper of our times. It's a go-to-war view of politics: the war is a just, unconditional-surrender war; the winner takes everything and the loser takes nothing.

It makes for the bitter politics that has divided our nation in half, that everyone complains about, but that all too few attempt to change. The view persists, not only between Democrats and Republicans, but among groups within the Democratic Party as well. It makes for bitter politics, but it makes for comfortable politics, too. It breeds political complacency and intellectual stand-pattism. You don't have to grapple seriously with the merits of conflicting ideas or philosophies or new facts; you dismiss them with a sneer or a scold.

It also produces a politics of fear—the fear of losing out or being shut out. This underlying fear has been largely responsible for blocking an honest discussion inside the Democratic Party over how to compose its future. Take the discussion about

values, for instance, which is critically related to the decisive political problem of how to recover the Party's traditional core, its
Jacksonian working-class base, especially blue-collar voters who
are white, since they are the ones who have left the fold.

Listening to the Republican rhetoric directed at working-
class whites during 2016, and noting its perhaps temporary
success, some Democrats feared that efforts to recapture traditional Democrats would necessarily lead to the imposition of
values, and perhaps especially racial values, that the Party had
struggled so mightily to overcome. This was hardly a realistic
fear—it was a thin caricature of millions of their fellow citizens—
but "I don't want their values in my party" was one conversation-
stopping response. Alternatively, one heard the progressive
argument that the Democratic Party was offering an economic-
policy program, and that if Jacksonians wished to return to
the party of their traditional heritage, economic policy was the
sole basis on which they would have to cast their ballots; otherwise, the discussion was off. The Jacksonians understandably
felt that the mainstream faction of the Democratic Party simply
didn't know them or the circumstances in which they found
themselves, wasn't interested in listening to them, was attempt-
ing to silence their instincts, maybe even feared and distrusted
them, and acted all too often to impose its nominees on their
communities. In this state of play, the Jacksonians were also
reluctant to renew the conversation. It's not going to be easy.

Democrats of all stripes have to find the courage to overcome
fears like these—and the mutual unfamiliarity that underlies
them. These are difficult questions, made more difficult by faulty
assumptions such as those just mentioned. They are hard questions, but they are not impossible ones to resolve. The Democrats have done it before, repeatedly. We need to face up to these

questions again today. We need to begin the New Conversation with a mighty determination to strengthen the Democratic Party by getting at the root causes of its current weaknesses. We did not get to work right after the 2016 elections. We need to get to work right now, right away.

The place to begin is at the beginning: the "northern tour" through New York and New England that Jefferson and Madison made in 1791, when they began to put together the public alliance that would become our political party. They were founding a party on the ethic of a shared faith in the dignity of the individual; a faith in the combined wisdom of the many as opposed to the handful; an explicit respect for differences in local conditions; and a deliberate determination to forge a coalition not only of disparate interests, but of disparate values as well. Virginia would not try to impose its values on Vermont, and Vermont would not try to impose its values on New York City. Jefferson and Madison and their new allies in the North realized it was going to look ragged, but they would show the will to work it out, because they knew they were losing the political argument of the day, and understood that only by cooperating across their manifest divisions would they be able to get what they wanted. It was not an anything-goes argument in 1791, of course, and it is not an anything-goes argument today. Instead, it is the argument that Adlai Stevenson made to the Democrats gathered in convention at Chicago in 1952, when he said: "We want no shackles on the mind or the spirit, no rigid patterns of thought, no iron conformity. We want only the faith and conviction that triumph in a free and fair contest."

A free and fair contest of ideas and ideals: this represents the best of our party, and the reality of its soul. No faction of the Party is going to succeed, ultimately, in willfully imposing its values wholesale on other cohorts of the Party that come out of different traditions or face different circumstances in making a go of it. That's a fact of life. All factions need to realize that the basic problem is to find a way to accommodate differing values within the common story we tell the country.

As a grand coalition of interests and ideals, Democrats face the fatal threat of domination by a single interest or a single ideal. Every time the danger of single-faction domination approaches reality inside the Democratic Party, we falter and fade as a national force. When southern slaveholders exercised an implicit veto over Democratic politics before the Civil War, we lost our ability to help save the Union, and were justly punished for fifty years afterward. When Bryan stood for justice on behalf of the beleaguered farmers of the Midwest and South, the emotion behind his cause was so great that it blotted out for a time other legitimate interests and ideals the Party had been standing for. The result was the great crossover election of 1896, which crippled our politics for nearly another twenty years.

We are beginning to look out-of-balance again today. Democrats return again and again to only half the ideals that made us the country's dominant political force for most of the past century. Especially we turn to the political myth of the faction in our party that carries by far the most weight today: the progressives with their faith in the value of public-policy arguments for the political battle, as well as for governing. This has become a problem.

As we think about the problem of Democratic politics today, we need to concentrate on the endgame of what we are trying to accomplish. We need to think first about where we want to take the country. That is the decisive question before the public in national debates. That is the way you mobilize a working political majority: around the issue of big goals, not around precise policy techniques. The goal is more important than the means of getting there. Yet our party has been lost in the details of policy for decades now. This is a politics of pointillism, the triumph of the technicality. It is a surefire formula leading straight to political paralysis. It commits a sin that is unpardonable in politics: it bores. Expertise is critical, but it cannot be allowed to rule the public contest. Purpose is the essence of politics. We need to emphasize goals, not techniques.

FDR's lesson from the New Deal is still valid, and today's Democrats should take it to heart. As to what, in the end, he needed to accomplish, FDR was firm. But as to the particular ways he would do it, he was entirely agnostic: with happy abandon, he freely mixed Hamilton with Jefferson, the private market with public regulation, Republican doctrine with Democratic, big business with small business. The goals of his politics were intentional and directional; the policies he adopted to advance his goals were a grab bag. The public rallied to him because it instinctively believed he would persist in service to his goals, no matter how. He became our most successful politician of the last century because of how he handled the end-purposes of what he was trying to do.

Democrats are now running the clear political peril of single-faction domination by the progressive wing of our party. The dominant faction is single-mindedly pressing not only its own interests on other factions of the Party, but its underlying values as well. It grates. This is not an argument for driving any faction from our party, and certainly not the progressives. Instead, it is an argument for rejecting domination by any single interest or ideal or narrow set of values.

We must break out and free our best impulses so as to reconstruct the grand coalition that allowed us to dominate American politics in the past. This cannot be done without solving the problem of how to recover the loyalty of the white working class. You can't keep claiming to be the party of the working class when great swaths of the working class vote against you, consistently and often overwhelmingly. This means that the Party must offer a secure space where this longest-sustaining element of the Democratic coalition can return to make the case for its legitimately American values, confident of the respect of its fellow Democrats. We don't need every single working-class voter; we probably couldn't get along with some of them. But we need a heavy majority of them. That's not going to be possible unless the Democratic Party demonstrates a deeper and more honest respect for the best and highest values of the Jacksonians: hard work, patriotism, spiritual core, individual dignity, straight truth-telling, mutual help in times of trouble. These are deep, authentic American values.

Ever since the battle over the Second Bank of the United States in 1832, the fight to help the outsider get inside the national mainstream has defined the purpose of the Democratic Party. From the Jacksonian Democracy down through the emergency of the Great Depression, our function in the life of the nation has been to stand for the outsider. This is our ideal of economic justice. We maintain a vague sort of public fealty to it today. But the truth is that since the end of Lyndon Johnson's determined Great Society efforts, we have too often become backsliders, slipping comfortably toward serving the well-off. Democrats have too long downplayed their responsibilities to the outsider. The new conversation has to include the need to strike a new balance. We must now return to our primary mission for justice in the economy.

The Jacksonian working class used to constitute the heart of Franklin Roosevelt's New Deal coalition. Many of its members have entirely legitimate complaints about how the American economy is working these days, and whose benefit it is working for. Countless workers in this group feel their chances slipping away, and it should be the business of the Democratic Party to see to it that they also, along with others, have the chance to make a dignified place for themselves and their families in this country.

During the last campaign, we either had no clear message to offer the Jacksonians in return for their support, or worse yet, we might have decided that we didn't care to offer such a message because we didn't want or need their support. These working-class voters punished us for our disregard, and even disdain, in 2016, with devastating effect. There was nothing unfair about what they did. This is the way a competitive democratic political system is supposed to work.

We have let them down. By allowing ourselves to become beguiled by the marvels of the new economy, we have too often forgotten the interests of the Jacksonians, and in doing so, we have turned our backs on the instincts and work of Jackson, and Wilson, and FDR, and LBJ. And Bryan—what would Bryan have said of the tidal wave of rural votes and evangelical votes that sank the Democratic Party's chances in the red Republican sea that spread across the nation's heartland in the fall of 2016? Are we now incapable of talking to America's farmers the way Truman talked to them in 1948? There is no reason why we should not be able to represent such interests honorably today. But the first thing we need to do is just to try. And that's a job that has to begin in our minds and hearts.

No one would suggest that Democrats now should pursue

only the interests of the white working class, and turn our attention away from our current supporters. We should be proud of the accomplishments we have achieved, and determined to remain loyal to the ideals and the interests of the communities that regularly support us. But the overall strategy we currently have clearly isn't working well enough. We need to add big new groups of supporters to our column. To do that, we need to place major emphasis on the kind of politics that worked for us so often in the past. This means making an argument that can unite working-class outsiders of all kinds under our banner. Our root political purpose is to fight for the outsider. Why would we want to limit ourselves to only certain kinds of outsiders?

We must hold for the outsider: all outsiders.

How we present our party to the larger public reflects a more important underlying reality, which is how we ourselves think about our own party. In the face of the troubles we have been having lately, various factions inside our party have been inviting Democrats to join a debate about whether we should continue our identity-politics paradigm, which sees the Party as a gathering of separate, often ethnically based factions, or whether we should endorse a more inclusive picture of our party based around unifying principles. This internal debate was explicitly joined during the 2016 campaign, and the identity-politics view prevailed among those who directed that effort.

Democrats should reject the invitation to join such a debate in the terms it has been offered: as a crude either-or proposition. Thomas Jefferson's "all men are created equal" credo, which is the emotional organizing ideal informing today's Democratic commitment to advancing new groups of Americans into the mainstream, is alive and strong inside the Party. It is what stands behind our commitment to civil rights and the constituency groups, including ethnic groups, that stand to benefit from this emphasis. The ideal is well understood by practically all of the rank and file, and it is not going to be dislodged. Sticking by our civil rights credo is the right thing to do for this country, and it's the politically advantageous thing to do for the Democratic Party. There is a legitimate place for identity politics in today's Democratic Party.

This is not, however, a sufficient basis for rejecting the opposing view outright. There may be Democrats with a strong commitment to civil rights who worry that abandoning our identity-politics prism will lessen the power of the civil rights allegiance of the Party. The opposite is true. The idea of a Democratic Party based on adherence to broad principles is not a formula for weakening the position of civil rights concerns within the Party. It is a formula for bringing new allies to that cause and strengthening our adherence to civil rights. Hyperspecific arguments in favor of hypernarrow policy solutions that touch only hyperdefined beneficiary groups can limit potential political support, and even repel those not directly affected. By contrast, the construction of an argument based on broad, general principle can afford people the chance to stand back a little, and to recognize their common interests, even though their precise circumstances may differ. Big concepts such as the fight for the outsider, the social gospel, economic growth and security, and the individual hold the prospect for sheltering many different kinds of interests and people and values under the same political banner, and for doing it with coherence and honor. The greatest of our leaders, practicing the best and highest politics, have always known that the key to success is an ability to articulate the larger public interest that can make sense out of the complexities of life.

Throughout the history of this country, Democrats have embraced different kinds of Americans and looked for political formulas that could not only unite these groups under our political party, but also bring them into the mainstream society of America itself. We have understood this to be part of our duty in following our political myth of the Fight for the Outsider, as well as Jefferson's "all men are created equal" credo.

The Republicans have a countermyth that they propound in opposition to these two Democratic myths: the myth of National Unity. It began with the attempt to impose "national unanimity" by passing the Alien and Sedition Acts, including the Naturalization Act, which targeted immigrants, in 1798, but it was massively and legitimately reinforced by the Republican Party's mighty efforts to save the Union in 1861–1865, and to reunite the country thereafter. The myth of National Unity is a very powerful one, stirring deep emotions, and it has enabled the Grand Old Party to enlist many voters in its cause, on many fronts, even when, arguably, their interests might not have comported with the ultimate purposes of the GOP.

These days, Democrats still celebrate difference. To a certain extent, this is a reflection of America's reality. The Jacksonian and Jeffersonian myths focus our attention on distinct and disadvantaged groups of Americans, but, like the other myths of the Democratic tradition, their true meaning is not static. These myths are dynamic. They are myths about change. They are political truths that contemplate people who can change their condition—and a country that can change its understandings of itself. They are fundamentally political myths about dynamic change, not about a snapshot in time.

Democrats have lately put a lot of focus on the starting lines of these political myths. Sometimes, perhaps inadvertently, we

have given the impression that this separateness at the start is
the only thing that our myths endorse: multiculturalism, internationalism, group identity in America. There's been a lot of
damaging political pushback. It's hard to win an argument with
someone who stakes out the high ground by trying to place an
exclusive claim on love of a unified country. We might conceive
of better terms on which to engage in this national discussion.
Without abandoning our commitments, we could become more
thoughtful about the other side of the Jeffersonian and Jacksonian ideals: the arrival into the American mainstream. Not
everyone wants to arrive in the mainstream, and that's all right,
but most people do. Democrats might put more thought than
they recently have to a celebration of the worthiness of the American mainstream, and how our party is committed to finding
ways for all Americans to arrive there, and find the tools they
need to succeed there. As Democrats, we can still celebrate difference, even as we open to the mainstream, and even as we remain skeptical of demands for outright, lockstep unity.

Democrats do understand, and follow, some parts of their
political myth these days—principally, Jefferson's "all men are
created equal" civil rights myth, FDR's New Deal economic-
security myth, and a modern and more narrow brand of the
original progressives' respect for ideas during Wilson's time.
We will maintain our hold on the ideals we follow. Nevertheless, the truth is that these three pillars of the Democratic faith
have not proved powerful enough, by themselves, to enable us
to regain control of the larger national political debate. We serve
about half of our originating ideals. We get about half of the
vote. We need more votes, and we need to look for them outside the encampments of our present supporters.

The best way to grow our party is to pay special attention to our founding political myths and ideals that we have neglected in the recent past. This means examining more thoughtfully the original Democratic ideals that might allow us to recapture the loyalty of those countless citizens who take great and justifiable pride in their innate American individualism; to reclaim the loyalty of large segments of the working class, and especially the most numerous white working class that has left home; and to make common cause with the public-spirited religious voters of this country, not only by inquiring after and serving their tangible interests, but also by showing respect for their values, which did so much to infuse our party with its innate instincts for altruism in the first place.

This is a strategy that can return votes by the million, instead of votes by the score. In the battle of ideals, we have been hesitant hangers-back of late. We should unlock our minds. We should fling open the windows. We should be more self-confident. We need to get more aggressive.

We need to create, for our own times, the common narrative that gives Democrats and potential Democrats good reason to enlist with us and stay with our party, even though they might come out of different intellectual traditions and understandings from the nation's past. As Democrats, we cannot continue to try to divide our way to victory by speaking separately and secretly to our separate constituency groups. It's unseemly. It demeans us. It demeans our supporters. We must destroy the silos into which we have compartmentalized our supporters. We must gather all Democrats into a public alliance with each other. We need one public, politically encompassing story that works for everyone. Emotional, simple, bold, understandable, and personal to each voter.

This is a story that must be told in ideals, and the Democratic ideals are difficult to put together with one another. In foreign policy, high ideals and hard interests; at home, economic security and individual initiative; throughout, expertise and popular sovereignty. Contradictions abound within each of these ideals; contradictions abound between them. We should embrace our contradictions instead of trying to hide them. We should find the ways that our contradictions can strengthen us, instead of allowing one or another Democrat to use these contradictions to pit us against each other. Democratic arguments for economic justice, for instance, can reach across the racial and ethnic barriers that so distressingly seem to divide people whose interests might otherwise coincide. The stories in this book illustrate how we can build a politics, both idealistic and coherent, based in political myths that might seem contradictory at first, but actually can be made compatible. They are tough to mesh coherently, but not impossible. We've done it before. We can do it again today.

THE NEW DEMOCRACY

Our political ancestors were serious about their ideas and their ideals and often fearless about serving them, and there is no reason why we should not be able to rise to our own occasion in the life of the Republic. It is our party now, ours to define according to the understandings of our times, for today and tomorrow— ours alone. But, in truth, we are not alone.

Basically, we are in a good position. When we stand for the dignity of the individual and fairness for the outsider, we are touching the most primal political instincts of our compatriots, as well as the philosophical taproots of our own party's origins.

When we respect the old words that speak the moral and religious impulses of our fellow countrymen pursuing reform in the secular realm, we are joining new and fruitful conversations that can bring us fresh and hopeful allies. In searching out and respecting the facts, we have hold of the critical temperament for figuring out how to build a better society. In placing the power of the common government behind the economic security of those who are in dire straits, we built the modern nation and still retain the loyalty of those who benefit even today. By inventing the Redeemer Nation marriage of ideals and interests, we established the dominant paradigm for American foreign policy. In serving the great goal of equality of all men and women, we are true to ourselves and soldiers in the fight for the coming America. In all of this, we, the Democrats, are the possessors of the very clay of political myth. And we hold in our hands the tools to fashion that clay into new organizational principles that can mobilize governing majorities of our fellow citizens.

But for us, there is one ideal that underlies all the others. Every chapter of this book is shot through with it. It is found in Jefferson's first words, the ethos that he and Jackson and all the Democrats who followed them fought so resolutely to expand ever since the beginning. The root principle is that *The People must rule*. This principle is always under attack, sometimes even by members of our own party. Today, the chatter can dwell on the dysfunction of our political system, on the hopelessness of our own fellow citizens and how power must be removed from them and placed in safer hands, guided by better-trained minds, producing faster, smarter results. Too many Democrats join this chorus, or at least such is the impression too many of our fellow citizens have received of us lately.

So we return at the end to where we started: The Democracy. It is our own principle as Democrats, our own meaning, the very chief end-purpose of our political party in the life of our country. Without this, at the last, we are nothing. That is why today's Democrats must emphatically renew our commitment to popular rule over the country and the government. If we fail in this, we shall become a strange and alien force in the life of the nation, and The People will exact a decisive retribution. To be true to ourselves, Democrats must actively look for every possible means to re-establish popular control, even when we might not agree with the particular and possibly temporary results.

And in our country, we need to recognize again that the political party itself is a weapon for popular rule in the hands of The People. The party stands separate from the government, and offers a parallel mechanism—and a very effective one—through which the populace can bring its views forcefully to bear on the government and those who hold elective office, or want to. The partisan's civic duty extends way beyond, and much deeper than, merely deciding whether to vote the party line on Election Day or dump it. A political party is a two-way street. It is meant to be used to enforce accountability.

The Democratic Party is a palpable institution made up of independent individuals. The Democrats who make up the Party—who *are* the Party—have the right to ask hard questions, and the ability to demand clarity from their suitors, and historically they also have a well-practiced record of disciplining their leadership by exerting popular control. But in appearing to lose interest in the workings of the Democratic Party recently, modern rank-and-file Democrats have in reality sacrificed this independent power that they once held in their hands.

When I started out in politics, I can remember sitting around late at night with political friends and candidates discussing election strategy, and somebody would suggest an idea for the fight, some position to adopt in the campaign. And so everyone in the back room would kick it around for a while, and then finally someone who had the respect of the group by virtue of really being in touch would say: "It might be a good idea, but the Party would never accept it." And that would be that: end of discussion. It doesn't happen anymore. The sense of the Democratic Party as an independent entity, a separate presence in the room, something apart that had to be seriously taken into account on its own—this sense is greatly diminished today. But it need not be.

This is not only a lesson about democracy in general; it is also a lesson about The Democracy, our political party. We have a responsibility to make The Democracy work, in the first place, so that American democracy can work.

One way to make The Democracy work is for rank-and-file Democrats to re-enter the Democratic Party structure—and then to use their positions to exert control over who is running for office, and what they are saying. The leadership of the Party is weak at the moment, which is the very thing that creates the opportunity for The People to step in. It is not true that everything must await the designation of the next Democratic nominee for president. The opposite is true. The time for rank-and-file Democrats to make their influence felt—with a thunderclap—is right now.

And a fundamental and critical part of making the Democratic Party work again is making sure our party delivers an understandable, coherent message that reflects the values and interests of our countrymen. Distracted by the machinations of politics and bewitched by the details of legislation and policy programs, the leadership of the Democratic Party, and its candidates and elected officials, have too often let go of the Party's core ideals. In doing so, they have drifted further and further from the citizenry whose votes they seek. What Jefferson, Jackson, Bryan, Wilson, FDR, and Truman all understood, and kept at the forefront of their minds, we must now learn again: every day, policies must be measured and held to account by the ideals they purport to serve. We need a politics conceived in the great political truths of our party; our ideals must come first. We have to think more clearly about who we are and what we believe in, down deep. We haven't been doing a good enough job of that.

Our ideals are what hold the promise for a reinvigorated and restored Party of The People. The People themselves are the ones who hold these seven core ideals of the Democratic Party in their hearts. The way to make sure that the Party puts its ideals front-and-center once more is for The People to take control of their political party again and reassert those ideals. Those ideals and political myths are the soul of the Democratic Party. They are the cornerstones for a new Democratic politics. They light the path back to power for the Democrats.

I look to The New Democracy.

ACKNOWLEDGMENTS

Every book has its friends, especially one that has had a long gestation period, as *Soul of a Democrat* has had. I must begin by expressing my heartfelt gratitude to Adam Bellow, editorial director of All Points Books at St. Martin's Press. Instinctively, he understood the concept of this book, and the special need for it in the current political climate. He understands how important it is to develop a new political conversation that merits the respect of the American people, and is determined to put All Points Books at the service of such a discussion, with authors from across the political spectrum. His suggestions for sharpening the focus of this work were acute. I also wish to thank his colleagues, Jennifer Weis at St. Martin's Press, and Kevin Reilly, at All Points, for their welcoming spirit.

My ruthless critic and now friend, Roger Labrie, was a superb editor for this book in the early stages, and I owe much to him for the clarity that he helped me bring to the manuscript, as well as his advice about the book-publishing world in general. Untold friends offered substantive ideas and criticisms, and there were many, also, who showed a deeply appreciated determination to help me find a way to get this book published. With sincere thanks, I should like to mention the following: James Dyett, John Herfort, Robin Moody, Anne Nelson, Ray Ottenberg, Tom Saenz, Rob Stein, Michael Thawley, Sandy Ungar. The staff of the Bender Library at the American University in Washington, D.C., were always helpful and unfailingly gracious to me as I was researching and writing this book—they are keepers of the flame. I want to thank my family, and especially my children, Laura and James Reston, who cheerfully entered so many dinner-table arguments about the politics of our country over so many years. Still, the debates about the Mexican-American War ring in my ears.

I have been lucky to have made numerous friends during my years in national politics, and although I bear the responsibility for the judgments I make here, the lessons they taught me appear throughout this book. But at the head of the line, I must pay my debt to the former chairman of the Democratic Party of Virginia, Senator Joseph T. Fitzpatrick of Norfolk.

Finally, I have dedicated this book to my late father, James B. Reston, who was Washington bureau chief and then executive editor of *The New York Times*, and who wrote a column on American politics and foreign policy in that newspaper for some forty years, winning the Pulitzer Prize twice. He was a superb journalist, and an even better dad. I hope that some of his spirit survives in these pages.

BIBLIOGRAPHIC NOTE

In my researching and writing of this book, I stand on the shoulders of giants.

I am deeply indebted to some of the great scholars of American political thought, and in particular to Richard Hofstadter, author of *The American Political Tradition* and *The Age of Reform*, for his lucid exposition of the formation and meanings of American political philosophy, and particularly of the period beginning with Bryanite populism and running through the New Deal. Also, V. L. Parrington, author of *Main Currents in American Thought*, especially for his olympian analysis of the seminal fight between Jefferson and Hamilton; and Arthur M. Schlesinger Jr., author of *The Age of Jackson*, for his acute analysis of the founding of the modern Democratic Party during the Jacksonian Democracy. Michael Kazin's biography of William Jennings Bryan, *A Godly Hero*, helped me recover a political figure too often dismissed. On Woodrow Wilson, aside from his own graceful crafting of his speeches and papers, I was much helped by August Heckscher's full-length life, *Woodrow Wilson:*

A Biography, and by James Chace's account of Wilson's thrilling first election in his book *1912*. On FDR, Frank Friedel, *Franklin D. Roosevelt: A Rendezvous with Destiny*; and on the Democrats' great domestic reforms during the Depression, William Leuchtenberg, *Franklin D. Roosevelt and The New Deal: 1932–1940*. *Truman*, by David McCullough. For a history of the intellectual currents of U.S. foreign policy, along with George Kennan's various works, there is none better than Walter Russell Mead's *Special Providence: American Foreign Policy and How It Changed the World*. Very useful to me, also, were the following: *Rendezvous with Destiny: A History of Modern American Reform*, by Eric Goldman; *The Rise of American Democracy: Jefferson to Lincoln*, by Sean Wilentz; *The Uprooted: The Epic Story of the Great Migrations That Made the American People*, by Oscar Handlin; *Party of The People: A History of the Democrats*, by Jules Witcover; *Democrats and the American Idea*, edited by Peter Kovler; and *Our Divided Political Heart*, by E. J. Dionne.

I thank them all, as well as the many other scholars whose works on political history and philosophy I consulted.